I0013254

INTRODUCTION

TO

ALGORITHMS

Understanding Data Structures and
Algorithms

THOMPSON CARTER

All rights reserved

No part of this book may be reproduced, distributed, or transmitted in any form or by any means without the prior written permission of the publisher, except in the case of brief quotations embodied in critical reviews and certain other noncommercial uses permitted by copyright law.

TABLE OF CONTENTS

INTRODUCTION

Algorithms: Understanding Data Structures and Algorithms"

In today's digital age, algorithms and data structures are foundational concepts that drive nearly every system we interact with on a daily basis. From the search engines we use to the social networks that keep us connected, to the autonomous vehicles that are reshaping our transportation systems, algorithms are behind the scenes, powering a wide range of applications. But for many, the concept of algorithms can seem abstract and overwhelming. How do they work? Why are they important? And most crucially, how do we design and implement them effectively?

This book aims to demystify algorithms and data structures by providing clear, jargon-free explanations and practical, real-world examples. We will take you step by step through the essential concepts, from understanding the basic building blocks to applying advanced algorithms in complex systems. Our goal is to equip you with a solid understanding of how algorithms work, how they are used to solve problems, and how to implement them efficiently in your own projects.

Why This Book Matters

In many fields, particularly in computer science, engineering, and software development, the ability to design and understand algorithms is an essential skill. Algorithms are essentially a set of well-defined instructions for solving problems or performing tasks. However, their importance extends far beyond theoretical applications—efficient algorithms can make the difference between a system that scales and performs well, and one that fails under pressure.

For example, when a social media platform scales to millions of users, the way it handles and retrieves user data through algorithms can directly impact its responsiveness and user experience. Similarly, in financial trading systems, the ability to compute complex models and predictions quickly can give companies a competitive edge. In healthcare, algorithms can assist in diagnosing diseases, predicting patient outcomes, and optimizing treatment plans, saving both time and lives.

Yet, despite their widespread use, many people still find it challenging to grasp algorithmic thinking, particularly when faced with complex problems. This book aims to break down these concepts into manageable chunks, using practical examples to show how these abstract ideas can be applied to solve real-world challenges.

What You Will Learn

In the chapters ahead, you will learn about the essential concepts and techniques that form the backbone of algorithmic design. We begin with the fundamentals, introducing data structures like arrays, linked lists, and hash tables—tools that help organize and store data efficiently. These are the building blocks upon which more complex algorithms are built.

From there, we move on to examining various types of algorithms that serve different purposes. You'll learn about:

- **Sorting algorithms** like QuickSort and MergeSort, which organize data into a specified order.
- **Search algorithms**, including binary search and hash-based searching, which allow us to efficiently find data in large sets.
- **Graph algorithms**, such as Dijkstra's algorithm and the A* search algorithm, which are used to solve problems in networks, routing, and pathfinding.
- **Dynamic programming** and **greedy algorithms**, two powerful paradigms that are used to solve optimization problems.
- **Backtracking** and **divide-and-conquer** approaches, which are used for breaking down problems into smaller, more manageable subproblems.

Through these topics, we will cover core algorithmic paradigms, including their time and space complexities, and provide insights into how to choose the right algorithm for a given problem. Along the way, you will also gain practical coding skills, as all the examples and exercises are accompanied by Python code snippets and explanations.

Real-World Applications and Case Studies

One of the most effective ways to understand the importance of algorithms is to see how they are applied in real-world scenarios. This book includes several case studies to illustrate how algorithms are used in industries ranging from e-commerce to healthcare to fintech.

- **E-Commerce and Recommendation Systems**: Learn how algorithms power recommendation engines that suggest products based on your browsing and purchasing history, enhancing the customer experience and driving sales.
- **Healthcare and Medical Algorithms**: Discover how machine learning algorithms are used to predict disease, diagnose medical conditions from images, and optimize treatment plans for patients.
- **Fintech and Fraud Detection**: Understand how algorithms detect fraudulent activities, predict financial risks, and

optimize investment strategies in the fast-paced world of finance.

- **AI and Machine Learning**: Explore how algorithms are the backbone of artificial intelligence, with applications in natural language processing, image recognition, and decision-making.

These real-world applications demonstrate how a deep understanding of algorithms and data structures is critical to solving complex problems, scaling systems, and driving innovation in a variety of industries.

The Structure of the Book

This book is divided into several parts, each focusing on a different aspect of algorithms and data structures.

- **Part I: Foundations of Algorithms** – In this section, we will introduce the basic principles of algorithm design, including the concept of algorithm complexity and the importance of choosing the right data structure for a given problem.
- **Part II: Fundamental Data Structures** – We delve deeper into essential data structures such as arrays, strings, linked lists, stacks, and queues. Understanding these structures will form the basis for more advanced algorithmic techniques.

- **Part III: Advanced Data Structures** – We explore more complex data structures such as trees, heaps, and graphs. These structures enable more efficient data storage and manipulation and are key to solving many algorithmic problems.

- **Part IV: Core Algorithm Paradigms** – In this section, we will explore common algorithmic strategies such as divide and conquer, backtracking, dynamic programming, and greedy algorithms. These paradigms provide systematic approaches to solving problems that are often encountered in software engineering and computational tasks.

- **Part V: Sorting, Searching, and Optimization Algorithms** – Here, we will focus on common algorithms for sorting data, searching through data structures, and solving optimization problems, essential skills for both software developers and data scientists.

- **Part VI: Advanced Topics and Applications** – In the final part of the book, we will look at advanced topics such as parallel and distributed algorithms, approximation and heuristic algorithms, and machine learning algorithms. These topics will expose you to the cutting edge of algorithmic development and help you understand how algorithms are evolving in the age of big data and artificial intelligence.

Who This Book Is For

This book is aimed at anyone who wants to gain a deeper understanding of algorithms and data structures, whether you're a beginner just starting out in programming, an intermediate programmer looking to enhance your problem-solving skills, or an experienced software developer seeking to brush up on your knowledge.

While the book is suitable for beginners, we avoid overwhelming technical jargon and focus on clear, accessible explanations. Each concept is accompanied by examples, exercises, and Python code snippets to help solidify your understanding. No prior knowledge of algorithms is required—just a basic understanding of programming will suffice.

Why Algorithms Matter

At its core, understanding algorithms is about solving problems efficiently. As data becomes more complex and systems scale, the need for optimized algorithms has never been greater. Whether you are building a mobile app, developing a machine learning model, or designing a financial system, the ability to choose and implement the right algorithm can make all the difference between success and failure.

Algorithms allow us to manage data more efficiently, improve user experiences, and build systems that can handle ever-increasing amounts of data. By understanding how algorithms work, you gain the ability to think critically about the problems you face and find the most effective solutions.

Final Thoughts

Algorithms are a cornerstone of computer science, and learning how to design, analyze, and implement them is a critical skill for any aspiring developer or data scientist. This book will give you the foundation you need to tackle complex problems, optimize solutions, and apply algorithmic thinking to real-world challenges.

By the end of this book, you'll not only understand how algorithms work, but also how to select the right algorithm for any problem, understand its strengths and limitations, and implement it effectively. With clear explanations, practical examples, and real-world applications, we aim to equip you with the tools you need to thrive in the rapidly evolving world of algorithms.

CHAPTER 1: INTRODUCTION TO ALGORITHMS

What are Algorithms, and Why Do They Matter?

In the most basic sense, an **algorithm** is a step-by-step procedure or set of instructions used to solve a problem or accomplish a task. Algorithms are the backbone of nearly every technological process, from simple calculations to complex machine learning models. They are foundational not only in computer science but across every field that requires data manipulation and decision-making, such as finance, healthcare, and engineering.

Why do algorithms matter?

1. **Efficiency:** Algorithms are about finding the most efficient way to solve a problem. This includes reducing the time it takes to process data (time complexity) and reducing the amount of memory or storage required (space complexity). For instance, sorting algorithms like quicksort or mergesort offer much better performance than simpler algorithms like bubble sort.

2. **Automation:** Algorithms automate tasks. For example, when you search for something on Google, the search engine uses an algorithm to find the most relevant results, rank them, and display them to you in fractions of a second.

3. **Optimization:** Algorithms help in optimization. Take navigation systems like Google Maps or GPS, where the algorithm calculates the fastest route from point A to point B. This real-time problem-solving involves dynamically adjusting the route based on traffic conditions or accidents, showcasing the importance of an algorithm in optimizing outcomes.

4. **Scalability:** Algorithms help systems scale. Whether handling large datasets or performing operations on millions of devices, well-designed algorithms are crucial for building systems that can handle growth without degrading performance.

In finance, for instance, algorithms are used in areas like fraud detection, stock market analysis, portfolio management, and even in making real-time trading decisions. Understanding how algorithms work, and how to design them, is central to leveraging computational power to solve complex problems efficiently.

Real-World Examples of Algorithms in Action

- **Google Search Engine:** When you enter a query into Google, it doesn't just search a database; it runs several complex algorithms that rank millions of web pages, select the most relevant, and present them in the correct order. This ranking is based on **PageRank**, a graph-based algorithm designed by Google's founders that evaluates the importance of web pages based on how they are linked to each other.

- **E-commerce Recommendation Systems:** When you shop on platforms like Amazon or Netflix, algorithms are analyzing your previous behavior (purchases, clicks, views) and comparing it with other users' behavior to suggest products or movies you may like. This uses algorithms in machine learning and data mining, such as collaborative filtering.

- **GPS Navigation Systems:** When you use apps like Google Maps or Waze, these apps use **Dijkstra's Algorithm** or *A search algorithm** to calculate the shortest or fastest route between two points, taking into account real-time data such as traffic, accidents, and road closures.

- **Healthcare Diagnostics:** In medical imaging, algorithms like edge detection and neural networks are used to identify tumors or abnormalities in X-ray and MRI scans. These algorithms assist doctors by identifying patterns in medical data that are often invisible to the human eye.

- **Social Media Algorithms:** Social media platforms like Facebook or Instagram use algorithms to decide which posts appear in your feed. These algorithms assess multiple factors, such as the time of the post, engagement (likes, comments, shares), and your interaction history with the poster to rank the relevance of posts.

These are just a few examples that illustrate the pervasive nature of algorithms. In every domain, from finance to healthcare to entertainment, algorithms are used to process data, make predictions, and automate decision-making processes.

How Algorithms and Data Structures Work Together

To understand algorithms fully, it's important to recognize the connection between **algorithms** and **data structures**. Data structures are specialized formats used to store, organize, and manage data. Algorithms operate on these data structures to solve problems efficiently.

For instance:

- In sorting algorithms like quicksort or mergesort, the array (or list) is the data structure that holds the data, and the algorithm works by repeatedly manipulating the array to arrange its elements in a specific order.
- In graph algorithms (e.g., **Dijkstra's Algorithm** for shortest paths), graphs are the data structure. These algorithms traverse the graph in a systematic way to find the solution.

Here's a simple analogy to clarify the relationship:

- **Data structures** are like containers for data, while **algorithms** are the tools or processes that manipulate that data inside the containers. For example, if you're organizing your bookshelf (a data structure), the algorithm would be the specific method you use to arrange the books (e.g., by genre, author, or title).

In practice, understanding which data structure to use in combination with a given algorithm is crucial for ensuring the program is efficient and scalable. For example, searching for a particular value in an unsorted list is best done using **linear search**, but with a **sorted list**, you can use **binary search**, which is much more efficient.

The Problem-Solving Process in Algorithm Design

Designing algorithms involves a structured problem-solving approach. Here's a breakdown of the process:

1. **Problem Definition:** Clearly define the problem. A good understanding of the problem ensures that you know the input and output, the constraints (e.g., time or space limitations), and the edge cases you must consider. In the case of sorting algorithms, the problem is clear: "Sort this list of numbers in ascending order."

2. **Designing the Algorithm:**

o **Brute Force:** Start with the simplest possible approach that solves the problem, even if it's not optimal. For example, a simple approach to sorting is the **bubble sort** algorithm, which repeatedly compares adjacent elements and swaps them if they are in the wrong order.

o **Optimization:** Once the brute force solution is in place, consider whether there are more efficient ways to solve the problem. This could involve reducing the time or space complexity, such as switching from bubble sort to quicksort for better performance on large datasets.

o **Divide and Conquer:** Break the problem into smaller subproblems. This is a key approach in many algorithms, such as merge sort or quicksort. Solving the subproblems independently and then combining their results can often lead to more efficient solutions.

o **Greedy Approach:** Sometimes, you can take a "greedy" approach where you make a series of choices, each of which seems best at the moment. Greedy algorithms are often used for optimization problems, like the **Knapsack Problem** or **Huffman Encoding**.

3. **Testing and Refining:** Once you have designed the algorithm, it is time to implement it and test it against sample input data. Look for edge cases (e.g., an empty list for sorting or negative numbers in a financial calculation) and optimize further if needed.

4. **Analysis:** Analyze the algorithm for **time complexity** (how long it takes to run) and **space complexity** (how much memory it uses). This analysis is crucial for ensuring that the algorithm will scale appropriately with larger datasets. For example, an algorithm with a time complexity of $O(n2)O(n^2)O(n2)$ will become much slower as the input size increases, whereas one with $O(nlogn)O(n \log n)O(nlogn)$ complexity will handle larger datasets much more efficiently.

Algorithms are powerful tools for solving real-world problems across various domains. Understanding the basic concepts of algorithm design and their relationship with data structures lays the foundation for more advanced algorithmic techniques. By mastering algorithm design and analysis, you can create efficient, scalable solutions that drive innovation in technology and many other fields. In this book, we will explore these algorithms and data structures in detail, providing practical examples and applications to help you apply what you've learned.

CHAPTER 2: UNDERSTANDING COMPLEXITY: BIG-O MADE SIMPLE

What is Algorithm Complexity?

Algorithm complexity refers to the measurement of how much time and space an algorithm takes to complete a task, given an input of a particular size. When we design algorithms, it's essential to understand how the performance of an algorithm scales as the input size increases. Complexity allows us to compare different algorithms based on their efficiency.

The two main types of complexity that we focus on are:

1. **Time Complexity:** This refers to how the running time of an algorithm changes as the size of the input grows. For example, if we double the size of the input, how does the execution time change? Time complexity gives us an estimate of the number of basic operations an algorithm will perform.

2. **Space Complexity:** This refers to how much memory (or space) an algorithm needs to solve a problem, relative to

the size of the input. Some algorithms might be time-efficient but memory-intensive, and vice versa.

Understanding both time and space complexity is crucial when designing algorithms, especially when working with large datasets or limited computational resources. By analyzing complexity, we can ensure that our algorithm performs well as data sizes grow.

Time Complexity vs. Space Complexity

While both time complexity and space complexity provide insights into an algorithm's efficiency, they address different concerns:

- **Time Complexity**: Focuses on the number of operations an algorithm performs. In terms of time, we analyze how the number of operations grows as the input size increases.

  Example: Consider an algorithm that performs a loop over an array of size nnn. Each iteration of the loop takes constant time, so the total time complexity would be $O(n)O(n)O(n)$, meaning the time grows linearly with the size of the input.

- **Space Complexity**: Focuses on the amount of memory used by the algorithm. This is important when dealing with large datasets or systems with limited memory.

Example: If an algorithm creates a new list or array to store data during execution, the space complexity reflects the size of that additional storage. If the algorithm needs space proportional to the input size, its space complexity might be $O(n)O(n)O(n)$.

In some cases, improving time complexity may come at the cost of higher space complexity, and vice versa. For example, a **recursive** algorithm might be more space-intensive due to function calls stacked in memory, but it might offer better performance (fewer operations) compared to an iterative approach.

Big-O, Big-Theta, and Big-Omega Explained

When analyzing algorithm complexity, we use several notations to describe the upper, lower, and tight bounds of an algorithm's performance. These notations allow us to understand how an algorithm behaves in the worst-case, best-case, and average-case scenarios:

1. **Big-O (O):** This is the most commonly used notation and describes the **upper bound** of an algorithm's running time. It tells us the worst-case scenario, or how bad the performance can get. When we say an algorithm has **O(n)** time complexity, it means that, in the worst case, the running time grows linearly with the size of the input.

   o **Example:** A linear search algorithm, which checks every element of an array to find a target, has a worst-case time complexity of $O(n)O(n)O(n)$, because in the worst case, it will look at every element in the array.

2. **Big-Theta (Θ):** This notation describes the **tight bound** of the algorithm's running time. Big-Theta gives both the upper and lower bounds of the algorithm's performance. It is used to represent algorithms whose performance is fairly consistent, regardless of the input.

   - **Example:** An algorithm that always processes each element of an array exactly once, like an **insertion sort** (in its best or worst form), has a time complexity of $Θ(n)\backslash Theta(n)Θ(n)$, meaning the time to complete the task grows linearly with the input size.

3. **Big-Omega (Ω):** This notation describes the **lower bound** of the algorithm's running time. It tells us the best-case scenario, or the minimum time required by the algorithm. For example, an algorithm with a best-case time complexity of $Ω(n)\backslash Omega(n)Ω(n)$ might take at least linear time, regardless of how optimized it is.

   - **Example:** For the **bubble sort** algorithm, the best case occurs when the list is already sorted. In this case, the time complexity is $Ω(n)\backslash Omega(n)Ω(n)$ because it still needs to iterate over the array at least once to confirm that it's sorted.

In summary:

- **Big-O** describes the **upper bound** (worst case).
- **Big-Theta** describes the **tight bound** (exact behavior).
- **Big-Omega** describes the **lower bound** (best case).

Each of these notations helps to define how an algorithm will behave under different conditions and provides insight into its efficiency.

Practical Examples: Sorting Algorithms and Their Complexities

Sorting is a fundamental problem in computer science, and analyzing the time and space complexity of sorting algorithms provides a great way to understand Big-O and related notations. Let's look at some common sorting algorithms and their complexities:

1. **Bubble Sort:**
   - **Time Complexity:** $O(n2)O(n^2)O(n2)$ in the worst case and $\Omega(n)\backslash Omega(n)\Omega(n)$ in the best case (if the list is already sorted).
   - **Space Complexity:** $O(1)O(1)O(1)$, because bubble sort sorts the array in place.
   - **Explanation:** Bubble sort repeatedly swaps adjacent elements that are out of order. It requires two nested loops, resulting in quadratic time complexity. In the best case (when the list is already

25

sorted), it only requires a single pass, making the best-case complexity $\Omega(n)$\Omega(n)$\Omega(n)$.

2. **Selection Sort:**

   o **Time Complexity:** $O(n2)O(n^2)O(n2)$ for both the best and worst cases.

   o **Space Complexity:** $O(1)O(1)O(1)$, as selection sort also sorts the array in place.

   o **Explanation:** Selection sort works by repeatedly finding the smallest (or largest) element from the unsorted part of the array and swapping it with the first unsorted element. Despite being simple, it still has quadratic time complexity, which makes it inefficient for large datasets.

3. **Merge Sort:**

   o **Time Complexity:** $O(n\log n)O(n \log n)O(n\log n)$ in the worst, best, and average cases.

   o **Space Complexity:** $O(n)O(n)O(n)$, because merge sort requires additional space for the temporary arrays used in the merge process.

   o **Explanation:** Merge sort is an efficient, divide-and-conquer algorithm. It divides the array into halves, recursively sorts them, and then merges the sorted halves. Its time complexity is logarithmic due to the divide-and-conquer approach, making it more efficient than bubble sort and selection sort for larger datasets.

4. **Quick Sort:**
   o **Time Complexity:** $O(n\log n)$ $O(n \log n)$ $O(n\log n)$ on average, but $O(n2)$ $O(n^2)$ $O(n2)$ in the worst case (when the pivot is poorly chosen).
   o **Space Complexity:** $O(\log n)$ $O(\log n)$ $O(\log n)$ due to recursion stack space.
   o **Explanation:** Quick sort is another divide-and-conquer algorithm, but instead of merging the halves like merge sort, it partitions the array around a pivot element. On average, quicksort performs better than merge sort because of better locality of reference and less memory usage.

Understanding algorithmic complexity is essential for evaluating the efficiency of different algorithms and choosing the right one for a particular problem. Time complexity helps us predict how algorithms perform as the size of the input grows, while space complexity ensures that we consider memory usage. By mastering Big-O, Big-Theta, and Big-Omega notations, you'll be able to analyze and compare algorithms with greater clarity, ensuring that your solutions are both efficient and scalable.

In this chapter, we've discussed the core concepts of algorithmic complexity and explored practical examples with sorting algorithms. In future chapters, we will dive deeper into other algorithms and data structures, continually analyzing their time and space complexities to build efficient problem-solving skills.

CHAPTER 3: THE BUILDING BLOCKS: DATA STRUCTURES

What are Data Structures, and Why Do We Need Them?

At the heart of computer science and programming, **data structures** are the fundamental building blocks that allow us to efficiently store, organize, and access data. In simple terms, a data structure is a way of organizing and storing data so that it can be accessed and modified efficiently. Think of them as containers that help us manage data in different forms.

Why are data structures so important? The efficiency of an algorithm depends significantly on how data is stored and manipulated. Without the right data structure, even the best algorithms can perform poorly. By choosing the correct data structure, we ensure that our algorithms run faster, require less memory, and are more scalable. This makes them essential not only in programming but also in real-world problem solving across various domains.

For instance, if you're building a social media platform, data structures are what allow you to efficiently store and retrieve user posts, comments, likes, and other interactions. They help optimize everything from loading your friend's news feed to sorting posts by relevance and timestamp.

Overview of Common Data Structures

There are several types of data structures, each designed to meet specific needs. Here's a brief overview of the most common ones:

1. **Arrays**:
   - **What are they?** An array is a fixed-size, ordered collection of elements, where each element is identified by an index.
   - **Why are they useful?** Arrays are fast for random access (i.e., you can quickly access any element by its index), but inserting or deleting elements can be slow.
   - **Example use case:** Storing a list of student grades in a class.

2. **Linked Lists**:
   - **What are they?** A linked list is a collection of nodes, where each node contains a value and a reference (or link) to the next node in the sequence.
   - **Why are they useful?** Linked lists allow for efficient insertions and deletions at both ends, but

accessing an element requires traversing the list from the beginning.

- o **Example use case:** Managing memory or implementing undo/redo functionality in applications.

3. **Stacks**:

- o **What are they?** A stack is a linear data structure that follows the Last In, First Out (LIFO) principle. The last element added is the first one to be removed.

- o **Why are they useful?** Stacks are used in scenarios where you need to keep track of a series of actions in reverse order, such as undo operations in a text editor or the function call stack in a program.

- o **Example use case:** Implementing a browser's back button functionality.

4. **Queues**:

- o **What are they?** A queue is a linear data structure that follows the First In, First Out (FIFO) principle. The first element added is the first one to be removed.

- o **Why are they useful?** Queues are ideal for scenarios where tasks need to be processed in the order they arrive, such as in task scheduling or managing requests in a web server.

o **Example use case:** Print job scheduling in a printer queue.

5. **Hash Tables**:

   o **What are they?** A hash table is a data structure that stores key-value pairs. A hash function computes an index where the corresponding value is stored.

   o **Why are they useful?** Hash tables provide fast access to data, allowing you to store and retrieve values in constant time, on average.

   o **Example use case:** Implementing a dictionary or a phonebook application where each name maps to a phone number.

6. **Trees**:

   o **What are they?** A tree is a hierarchical structure consisting of nodes, with each node containing a value and references to child nodes.

   o **Why are they useful?** Trees are useful for organizing data in a way that enables fast searching, insertion, and deletion. They are widely used in databases, file systems, and search engines.

   o **Example use case:** File systems, where each folder is a node and files within folders are child nodes.

7. **Graphs**:

   o **What are they?** A graph is a collection of nodes (vertices) and edges that connect pairs of nodes.

Graphs can be either directed (edges have direction) or undirected (edges have no direction).

- o **Why are they useful?** Graphs are ideal for representing relationships between entities, such as networks, social connections, and routes in a city.
- o **Example use case:** Social networks (friendship relations) or transportation networks (connecting cities).

How Algorithms Leverage Data Structures

Data structures play a critical role in the design and performance of algorithms. An algorithm is essentially a step-by-step process for solving a problem, and the way we store and access the data in that problem can drastically affect how efficiently the algorithm works. Here's how some common algorithms leverage specific data structures:

1. **Searching Algorithms**:
   - o Searching algorithms like **binary search** are optimized by using **sorted arrays** or **binary search trees (BSTs)**. For example, binary search operates on a sorted array to find an element in logarithmic time $(O(\log n)O(\log n)O(logn))$, whereas linear search works on an unsorted list and has a time complexity of $O(n)O(n)O(n)$.

2. **Sorting Algorithms**:

- o Sorting algorithms such as **quick sort** or **merge sort** rely on **arrays** for efficient data manipulation. The array's contiguous memory structure makes it easier to divide and conquer the data, leading to more efficient sorting algorithms (e.g., $O(n\log n)$ for merge sort).

3. **Graph Algorithms**:
   - o **Dijkstra's algorithm** for finding the shortest path in a graph uses **priority queues** (often implemented with heaps) to store the vertices with the smallest tentative distance. **Depth-first search (DFS)** and **breadth-first search (BFS)** utilize **stacks** and **queues**, respectively, to traverse the graph.

4. **Dynamic Programming**:
   - o Many dynamic programming algorithms (e.g., the **knapsack problem**) rely on **arrays** or **hash tables** to store intermediate results (memoization), which allows for efficient lookup and avoids redundant computation.

By selecting the right data structure, you can ensure that your algorithm is as efficient as possible in terms of both time and space. In fact, one of the key challenges in algorithm design is choosing the right data structure to solve the problem at hand.

Real-World Analogy: Libraries and Bookshelves

A helpful way to understand data structures is through a real-world analogy. Think of **data structures** as **libraries** and **bookshelves** that store information. Here's how it works:

- **Array as a Bookshelf**: Imagine you have a bookshelf where the books are organized by index (i.e., each book has a specific position). If you know the index, you can easily grab the book you want. This is similar to how arrays store elements at fixed positions. The drawback is that adding or removing books in the middle of the shelf can be cumbersome, much like arrays' inefficiency with insertions or deletions.

- **Linked List as a Chain of Books**: Now, think of each book being chained together by a string. You can easily add new books to the collection, but to find a specific book, you must start at the beginning and follow the chain. This is how linked lists work: while they make it easy to insert or remove books (nodes), accessing them can take longer.

- **Queue as a Library Checkout Line**: A queue works like the checkout line in a library. The first person to enter the line is the first to be served. If you're at the front of the line, you can check out a book; if you're at the back, you'll have to wait. This is how queues operate—tasks are processed in the order they arrive.

- **Stack as a Stack of Books**: A stack is like a pile of books where you can only add or remove the top book. To access a book, you need to remove the ones above it first. This mirrors the "Last In, First Out" (LIFO) principle of stacks.

- **Hash Table as a Library Catalog**: Think of a library catalog system where each book has a unique identifier (like a book ID). Using this identifier, you can instantly find the book's location on the shelf. This is similar to a hash table, where data is stored in key-value pairs and can be quickly retrieved using a hash function.

- **Tree as a Library's Classification System**: Imagine a library that organizes its books by subject, author, and title in a hierarchical way. At the top of the structure, there are broad categories (like Fiction, Non-Fiction), and within each, there are subcategories. This mirrors a **tree** data structure, where nodes branch out into other nodes, representing a hierarchy of relationships.

Data structures are the backbone of computer algorithms and essential for efficient data manipulation. Choosing the right data structure can significantly impact the performance of your algorithms, especially as the input data grows in size. By understanding the core data structures—arrays, linked lists, stacks, queues, hash tables, trees, and graphs—you gain the foundational knowledge needed to tackle complex problems and design efficient solutions.

In this chapter, we've explored the various types of data structures, how they are used in algorithm design, and provided real-world analogies to clarify their importance. In subsequent chapters, we will dive deeper into each data structure, examining their complexities and real-world applications in greater detail.

CHAPTER 4: RECURSION: BREAKING PROBLEMS INTO SMALLER PIECES

Understanding the Concept of Recursion

At its core, **recursion** is a problem-solving technique where a function calls itself in order to solve a smaller version of the original problem. The key idea is that complex problems can be broken down into simpler subproblems, and by solving these subproblems recursively, you can eventually solve the entire problem.

In a recursive function, two main elements are typically involved:

1. **Base Case**: This is the simplest, smallest version of the problem, which can be solved directly without further recursion. It's necessary to prevent the function from calling itself indefinitely (i.e., infinite recursion).

2. **Recursive Case**: This is where the function breaks the problem down into smaller subproblems, calling itself with

the reduced problem. Each recursive call should ideally make progress towards reaching the base case.

Recursion is particularly useful for problems that involve repetitive subproblems, hierarchical structures, or problems that can be divided into smaller, identical tasks. Many algorithms, especially those involving trees, graphs, and divide-and-conquer strategies, are naturally recursive.

Real-Life Examples of Recursion

To understand recursion better, let's consider a few real-life analogies that illustrate how this concept works:

1. **Russian Dolls (Nested Dolls)**: Think of **Russian dolls** (matryoshka dolls), where one doll contains another, and each smaller doll contains an even smaller one. The process of opening a Russian doll is recursive:
    o   Open the outermost doll (recursive call).
    o   Inside it, there is another doll, and you repeat the process (recursive call).
    o   Eventually, you reach the smallest doll, which does not contain another doll, and the recursion ends (base case).

In this analogy, the act of opening dolls mimics a recursive function, where each step works on a smaller version of the original problem, and the base case is when you find the innermost doll.

2. **Tree Traversal**: Imagine you are exploring a tree, where each branch might have more branches, and each branch might have leaves at the end. The process of walking through the tree is recursive:

    o First, you look at the current node (root).

    o Then, you recursively explore the left subtree.

    o After finishing with the left subtree, you explore the right subtree.

    o If a node has no children (i.e., it's a leaf), the recursion ends at that node (base case).

This is a classic case of recursion in computer science—traversing a tree or a hierarchical structure.

3. **Factorial Calculation**: The factorial of a number nnn is the product of all positive integers less than or equal to nnn. It can be defined recursively:

    o $n!=n\times(n-1)!n! = n \times (n-1)!n!=n\times(n-1)!$, for $n>1n > 1n>1$

    o The base case is $1!=11! = 11!=1$

In this case, each recursive call reduces nnn by 1 until reaching the base case.

Writing Recursive Algorithms

Let's take a look at how to write a recursive algorithm. We'll start with a simple example: **calculating the factorial of a number**.

Example 1: Factorial Function in Python

python

```python
def factorial(n):
    # Base case: if n is 1, return 1
    if n == 1:
        return 1
    # Recursive case: multiply n by the factorial of (n-1)
    else:
        return n * factorial(n - 1)
```

In this function:

- The **base case** is when nnn equals 1, in which case the function returns 1 (since $1!=11! = 11!=1$).
- The **recursive case** calls the function again with n−1n - 1n−1, reducing the problem until it reaches the base case.

Example Output:

python

```python
print(factorial(5))  # Output: 120
```

The calculation follows this recursive breakdown:

- 5!=5×4!5! = 5 \times 4!5!=5×4!
- 4!=4×3!4! = 4 \times 3!4!=4×3!
- 3!=3×2!3! = 3 \times 2!3!=3×2!
- 2!=2×1!2! = 2 \times 1!2!=2×1!
- 1!=11! = 11!=1 (base case)

Thus, 5!=5×4×3×2×1=1205! = 5 \times 4 \times 3 \times 2 \times 1 = 1205!=5×4×3×2×1=120.

Example 2: Fibonacci Sequence

Another common example of recursion is calculating the **Fibonacci sequence**, where each number is the sum of the two preceding ones. The sequence starts as follows: 0, 1, 1, 2, 3, 5, 8, 13, ...

Here's the recursive formula:

- F(n)=F(n−1)+F(n−2)F(n) = F(n-1) + F(n−2)F(n)=F(n−1)+F(n−2) for n>1n > 1n>1
- The base cases are F(0)=0F(0) = 0F(0)=0 and F(1)=1F(1) = 1F(1)=1

python

```
def fibonacci(n):
    # Base cases: return n if it's 0 or 1
    if n == 0:
```

```
    return 0
elif n == 1:
    return 1
# Recursive case: F(n) = F(n-1) + F(n-2)
else:
    return fibonacci(n - 1) + fibonacci(n - 2)
```

Example Output:

python

```
print(fibonacci(6))  # Output: 8
```

The recursion breaks down as:

- $F(6)=F(5)+F(4)F(6) = F(5) + F(4)F(6)=F(5)+F(4)$
- $F(5)=F(4)+F(3)F(5) = F(4) + F(3)F(5)=F(4)+F(3)$
- And so on, until the base cases are reached.

Common Pitfalls: Infinite Recursion and Stack Overflow

While recursion is a powerful technique, it is not without its challenges. Two common issues that arise in recursive algorithms are **infinite recursion** and **stack overflow**.

1. **Infinite Recursion**: Infinite recursion occurs when the base case is never met, causing the function to call itself endlessly. This often happens if the problem is not reduced correctly or the base case is missing.

Example of infinite recursion:

python

```
def infinite_recursion(n):
    # Missing base case!
    return infinite_recursion(n - 1)  # This will never stop!
```

In this case, the function keeps calling itself with decreasing values of nnn and never reaches a base case, leading to infinite recursion.

Solution: Ensure that your recursion always makes progress toward reaching the base case, and the base case should terminate the recursion.

2. **Stack Overflow**: A stack overflow happens when the recursion depth is too large, causing the program to run out of memory. In languages like Python, each recursive call adds a new frame to the call stack, and if the recursion is too deep, the stack will exceed its limit.

Example of stack overflow:

python

```
def deep_recursion(n):
```

return deep_recursion(n + 1) # Recursively calls itself endlessly

Solution: Limit the depth of recursion by ensuring that the base case is reached before the recursion depth becomes too large. In some cases, you may need to refactor your recursive algorithm into an iterative one to prevent stack overflow.

Recursion is a powerful and elegant way to solve problems, particularly those that involve repetitive subproblems or hierarchical structures. By breaking down a complex problem into smaller, more manageable pieces, recursion can simplify the design of algorithms, making them more intuitive and easier to implement.

While recursion can be a tricky concept to master, understanding the basic principles of the base case, recursive case, and ensuring progress toward the base case is essential to writing effective recursive functions. Additionally, being aware of pitfalls such as infinite recursion and stack overflow can help avoid common errors in recursive algorithms.

In the next chapter, we will explore **iterative solutions** to problems typically solved with recursion, and discuss how to choose between the two approaches based on the problem at hand.

CHAPTER 5: ARRAYS AND STRINGS

Basics of Arrays and Their Operations

At the heart of computer science, **arrays** are one of the most fundamental data structures. They provide a way to store multiple values of the same type in a contiguous block of memory. Arrays are used in a wide range of applications due to their simplicity, fast access times, and their ability to hold collections of elements.

Definition: An array is a collection of elements, each identified by an index or a key. The elements are stored in contiguous memory locations, meaning that the memory addresses of the elements are consecutive.

Key Properties of Arrays:

- **Fixed Size**: Once an array is created, its size is determined and cannot be changed. This means that the number of elements it can hold is fixed.

- **Indexing**: Elements in an array are accessed using an index. In most programming languages, the index starts at 0. For example, the first element is accessed via index 0, the second element via index 1, and so on.

- **Efficient Access**: Arrays offer **constant time access** to their elements, i.e., $O(1)O(1)O(1)$ time complexity for reading or writing an element at a given index.

- **Homogeneity**: All elements of an array are of the same type (e.g., all integers, all strings), which simplifies storage and access patterns.

Common Array Operations:

1. **Accessing an Element**: Use the index to access an element in constant time.

python

```
arr = [1, 2, 3, 4]
print(arr[2])  # Output: 3
```

2. **Inserting an Element**: Inserting an element into an array is efficient only if you're adding it at the end (amortized

O(1)O(1)O(1)). If you want to insert at a specific index, it takes O(n)O(n)O(n) due to the need to shift elements.

python

```
arr = [1, 2, 3]
arr.insert(1, 4)  # Insert 4 at index 1
print(arr)  # Output: [1, 4, 2, 3]
```

3. **Deleting an Element**: Deleting an element also requires shifting elements if you're not deleting from the end.

python

```
arr = [1, 2, 3, 4]
arr.pop(1)  # Removes the element at index 1
print(arr)  # Output: [1, 3, 4]
```

String Manipulation as a Type of Array Problem

A **string** in most programming languages is essentially an array of characters. Each character in the string is stored as an individual element, with the string providing a way to access each character by its index.

Common String Operations:

1. **Substring Search**: Searching for substrings in a string is a classic example of string manipulation. A well-known algorithm for this task is the **Knuth-Morris-Pratt (KMP)** algorithm, which efficiently searches for a substring within a larger string.

2. **Reversing a String**: Reversing a string involves swapping characters from opposite ends, which can be implemented using array manipulation techniques.

3. **Pattern Matching**: Pattern matching involves searching for occurrences of a specific pattern (a substring or a sequence of characters) within a larger string. This can be done efficiently using algorithms such as **Rabin-Karp** or **Boyer-Moore**.

Example: Checking if a String is Palindromic: A palindromic string reads the same forward and backward. We can check if a string is palindromic by comparing the first half of the string with the reverse of the second half.

python

```python
def is_palindrome(s):
    return s == s[::-1]


print(is_palindrome("racecar"))  # Output: True
```

In this example, the string s[::-1] uses Python's slicing syntax to reverse the string. The check s == s[::-1] determines whether the string is palindromic.

Applications: Substring Search, Text Processing

1. **Substring Search**: A classic problem in text processing is finding all occurrences of a substring within a string. A naive solution would involve checking each possible starting position in the string, which can be inefficient for large strings. Instead, more advanced algorithms like **KMP**, **Boyer-Moore**, and **Rabin-Karp** can be used for more efficient substring searching.

   KMP Algorithm:

   o The Knuth-Morris-Pratt (KMP) algorithm improves upon the brute-force approach by using information about the pattern itself to skip over unnecessary comparisons. It precomputes a "partial match" table to avoid rechecking characters that have already been matched.

   Example of KMP algorithm for substring search:

   python

```python
def KMPSearch(text, pattern):
    m, n = len(pattern), len(text)
    lps = [0] * m  # Longest prefix suffix array
    j = 0  # index for pattern

    # Preprocess the pattern (calculate lps array)
    computeLPSArray(pattern, m, lps)

    i = 0  # index for text
    while i < n:
        if pattern[j] == text[i]:
            i += 1
            j += 1

        if j == m:
            print(f"Pattern found at index {i - j}")
            j = lps[j - 1]

        elif i < n and pattern[j] != text[i]:
            if j != 0:
                j = lps[j - 1]
            else:
                i += 1
```

2. **Text Processing**: Text processing, such as **text tokenization**, **counting word frequencies**, and **finding occurrences of specific words** in a document, often relies on efficient use of arrays and strings. For instance, tokenization is the process of splitting a text into words or phrases, and it can be done by iterating through a string and storing tokens in an array.

Example: Counting word frequencies:

python

```
from collections import Counter
text = "the quick brown fox jumps over the lazy dog"
words = text.split()  # Split the text into a list of words
word_count = Counter(words)  # Count the occurrences of each word
print(word_count)  # Output: Counter({'the': 2, 'quick': 1, 'brown': 1, 'fox': 1, 'jumps': 1, 'over': 1, 'lazy': 1, 'dog': 1})
```

Optimizations and Real-World Examples (e.g., Autocomplete)

One of the most practical applications of arrays and strings is in **autocomplete** systems, such as those used in search engines, IDEs, and text editors. Autocomplete suggests possible completions based on the user's current input, and it can be optimized using **trie data structures** or **prefix trees**.

51

1. **Autocomplete with Arrays and Strings**: The autocomplete algorithm typically stores a set of valid suggestions in a data structure like a **trie**. As a user types a string, the algorithm matches the prefix of the current input with stored words in the trie, offering possible completions.

2. **Optimizing with Tries**: A **trie** is a tree-like data structure that stores strings in a way that allows for efficient prefix matching. Each node in the trie represents a character, and the path from the root to a node represents a prefix of a word in the dataset.

Example: Autocomplete with a Trie:

python

```python
class TrieNode:
    def __init__(self):
        self.children = {}
        self.is_end_of_word = False


class Trie:
    def __init__(self):
        self.root = TrieNode()

    def insert(self, word):
        node = self.root
```

```python
        for char in word:
            if char not in node.children:
                node.children[char] = TrieNode()
            node = node.children[char]
        node.is_end_of_word = True

    def search(self, prefix):
        node = self.root
        for char in prefix:
            if char not in node.children:
                return []
            node = node.children[char]
        return self._get_words_with_prefix(node, prefix)

    def _get_words_with_prefix(self, node, prefix):
        words = []
        if node.is_end_of_word:
            words.append(prefix)
        for char, child_node in node.children.items():

words.extend(self._get_words_with_prefix(child_node,
prefix + char))
        return words
```

With this **Trie** structure, you can efficiently retrieve all words that share a common prefix, making it ideal for implementing an autocomplete feature.

Arrays and strings are fundamental data structures in computer science, and understanding how to manipulate them efficiently is crucial for solving many practical problems in software development. From searching and sorting to more advanced applications like autocomplete and text processing, these structures play a critical role in algorithm design.

In this chapter, we've explored the basics of arrays, the ways strings are treated as arrays, and how operations like substring search, pattern matching, and text processing can be performed efficiently. We've also looked at real-world optimization techniques and examples, like autocomplete, where arrays and strings are used in combination with more advanced data structures like tries to achieve fast and scalable solutions.

In the next chapter, we'll dive into **Linked Lists**, another fundamental data structure that enables more dynamic memory management and efficient insertion/deletion operations compared to arrays.

CHAPTER 6: LINKED LISTS

Introduction to Linked Lists

A **linked list** is a linear data structure where each element (or node) points to the next element in the sequence. Unlike arrays, which store elements in contiguous memory locations, a linked list consists of a collection of nodes, where each node contains data and a reference (or link) to the next node in the sequence. This flexibility makes linked lists particularly useful for dynamic memory allocation, where the size of the list can change during runtime without the need for resizing.

While arrays are great for random access and constant-time lookups, linked lists excel in scenarios that require efficient insertion and deletion operations, especially when dealing with large datasets or data structures that change frequently.

Types of Linked Lists

1. **Singly Linked List**: In a singly linked list, each node contains:
   - o **Data**: The actual value of the node.
   - o **Next pointer**: A reference to the next node in the list.

The list starts with a **head** node, and each node points to the next node in the sequence, with the last node pointing to None (indicating the end of the list).

Example:

python

```
class Node:
    def __init__(self, data):
        self.data = data
        self.next = None


class SinglyLinkedList:
```

```
def __init__(self):
    self.head = None

def append(self, data):
    new_node = Node(data)
    if not self.head:
        self.head = new_node
    else:
        current = self.head
        while current.next:
            current = current.next
        current.next = new_node

def display(self):
    current = self.head
    while current:
        print(current.data, end=" -> ")
        current = current.next
    print("None")
```

Operations:

o **Insertion**: To insert a node at the beginning, middle, or end, we simply adjust the next pointers.

o **Deletion**: To delete a node, we adjust the previous node's next pointer to skip over the node being removed.

2. **Doubly Linked List**: In a doubly linked list, each node has two pointers:

   o **Next pointer**: A reference to the next node.

   o **Previous pointer**: A reference to the previous node.

This allows for bidirectional traversal, making it easier to move both forward and backward through the list. A doubly linked list also has a **head** and **tail** pointer, where the head points to the first node and the tail points to the last node, which is useful for efficiently adding nodes at both ends.

Example:

python

```python
class DoublyNode:
    def __init__(self, data):
        self.data = data
        self.next = None
        self.prev = None


class DoublyLinkedList:
    def __init__(self):
        self.head = None

    def append(self, data):
```

```
new_node = DoublyNode(data)
if not self.head:
    self.head = new_node
else:
    current = self.head
    while current.next:
        current = current.next
    current.next = new_node
    new_node.prev = current

def display(self):
    current = self.head
    while current:
        print(current.data, end=" <-> ")
        current = current.next
    print("None")
```

3. **Circular Linked List**: A circular linked list is similar to a singly or doubly linked list, except that the last node points back to the head, creating a circular reference. In a **singly circular linked list**, the last node's next pointer points to the first node, while in a **doubly circular linked list**, the next pointer of the last node points to the first, and the prev pointer of the first node points to the last node.

Example of a **Singly Circular Linked List**:

python

```python
class CircularNode:
    def __init__(self, data):
        self.data = data
        self.next = None


class CircularLinkedList:
    def __init__(self):
        self.head = None

    def append(self, data):
        new_node = CircularNode(data)
        if not self.head:
            self.head = new_node
            new_node.next = self.head
        else:
            current = self.head
            while current.next != self.head:
                current = current.next
            current.next = new_node
            new_node.next = self.head

    def display(self):
        if not self.head:
```

```
        return
    current = self.head
    while True:
        print(current.data, end=" -> ")
        current = current.next
        if current == self.head:
            break
    print("...")
```

Operations on Linked Lists

1. **Insertion**: Insertion in a linked list involves creating a new node and adjusting the pointers accordingly. There are three types of insertions:

   o **At the Beginning**: Set the new node's next pointer to the current head, and then update the head to the new node.

   o **At the End**: Traverse to the last node and adjust its next pointer to point to the new node.

   o **In the Middle**: Traverse to the node after which the new node should be inserted and adjust the pointers.

Example: Inserting at the beginning:

python

```python
def insert_at_beginning(self, data):
    new_node = Node(data)
    new_node.next = self.head
    self.head = new_node
```

2. **Deletion**: Deletion involves removing a node from the list and adjusting the pointers of adjacent nodes to bypass the deleted node. There are three types of deletions:

    o **From the Beginning**: Set the head pointer to the second node in the list.

    o **From the End**: Traverse the list to find the second-last node, then set its next pointer to None.

    o **From the Middle**: Traverse to the node just before the one to be deleted and adjust its next pointer to skip the node.

Example: Deleting the first node:

python

```python
def delete_first(self):
    if self.head:
        self.head = self.head.next
```

3. **Traversal**: Traversing a linked list involves visiting each node in sequence, starting from the head, and performing

some operation (like printing or modifying) on the node data.

Example: Traversing and printing all elements:

python

```
def traverse(self):
    current = self.head
    while current:
        print(current.data, end=" -> ")
        current = current.next
    print("None")
```

Use Cases of Linked Lists

1. **LRU (Least Recently Used) Cache**: An LRU cache is a data structure used to store a fixed number of items, with the least recently used item being evicted when the cache is full. A linked list is often used in combination with a hash map to implement an efficient LRU cache.
   - o **Doubly Linked List**: Nodes are moved to the front of the list when they are accessed, and the least recently used node is removed from the back.
   - o **Hash Map**: A hash map allows quick lookup of the nodes by key.

Example:

python

```python
class LRUCache:
    def __init__(self, capacity):
        self.cache = {}
        self.capacity = capacity
        self.order = DoublyLinkedList()

    def get(self, key):
        if key in self.cache:
            self.order.move_to_front(key)
            return self.cache[key]
        return -1

    def put(self, key, value):
        if len(self.cache) >= self.capacity:
            self.evict()
        self.cache[key] = value
        self.order.add_to_front(key)
```

2. **Undo Functionality in Text Editors**: Linked lists can be used to manage **undo** functionality in text editors, where each node represents a state of the document. When the user presses undo, the system moves backward in the

linked list to retrieve the previous state. A **doubly linked list** is useful here because it allows both forward and backward navigation.

Example:

python

```python
class TextEditor:
    def __init__(self):
        self.history = DoublyLinkedList()
        self.current = None

    def type(self, text):
        self.history.append(self.current)
        self.current = text

    def undo(self):
        if self.history.head:
            self.current = self.history.head.data
            self.history.head = self.history.head.next
```

Comparison with Arrays: Strengths and Limitations

1. **Strengths of Linked Lists**:

o **Dynamic Size**: Linked lists are dynamic, meaning they can grow or shrink in size without the need to allocate a contiguous block of memory, unlike arrays.

o **Efficient Insertions/Deletions**: Linked lists are particularly efficient when inserting or deleting elements, especially in the middle of the list, because there is no need to shift elements like in an array.

o **Memory Efficiency**: Linked lists do not require a pre-allocated block of memory and only use the memory necessary for each node, unlike arrays which require a fixed size.

2. **Limitations of Linked Lists**:

o **Access Time**: Linked lists have slower access times than arrays because nodes are not stored in contiguous memory locations. To access an element, you must traverse the list from the beginning, which takes linear time.

o **Extra Memory for Pointers**: Each node in a linked list requires additional memory to store the pointer(s), making linked lists less memory-efficient than arrays in terms of overhead.

Linked lists are a fundamental data structure that forms the basis for many more complex data structures and algorithms. Understanding linked lists, their variations, and their operations is crucial for anyone diving deeper into algorithms and data structures. Whether you're implementing caches, undo functionality, or more advanced structures like queues and stacks, mastering linked lists will provide the flexibility needed for efficient memory management and dynamic data handling.

CHAPTER 7: HASH TABLES

What Are Hash Tables, and How Do They Work?

A **hash table** (or hash map) is a data structure that implements an **associative array** abstract data type, a structure that can map keys to values. Hash tables allow for efficient data retrieval based on a key, providing near-constant time complexity **O(1)** for lookups, insertions, and deletions, assuming the hash function distributes keys well. The key idea behind a hash table is the **hash function**, which takes an input (the key) and returns an index (the hash) in a list (the array). This index determines where the associated value should be stored.

At the core of a hash table, you have two main components:

1. **Keys**: The identifiers used to store and retrieve values.
2. **Values**: The data that you want to store and retrieve associated with a particular key.

Basic Operations in Hash Tables

- **Insertion**: Adding a key-value pair to the hash table.
- **Lookup/Searching**: Retrieving a value using a key.
- **Deletion**: Removing a key-value pair from the table.
- **Updating**: Modifying the value associated with an existing key.

A well-designed hash table ensures that these operations are performed in constant time, **O(1)**, on average, but this depends on the quality of the hash function and how collisions are handled.

Real-Life Analogy: Associative Memory

A real-life analogy for a hash table is a **phonebook** or a **dictionary**. In a phonebook, you can quickly look up someone's phone number by searching for their name. The **name** is the **key**, and the **phone number** is the **value**. This lookup is efficient because the names (keys) are indexed in a way that allows you to quickly find the phone number (value) associated with that name.

Similarly, in a **dictionary**, words are associated with definitions. The words are the keys, and the definitions are the values. If you want to find the definition of a word, you can look it up by its key (the word), which makes searching for a definition much faster than going through a list of words one by one.

Hash Functions and Collision Handling

A **hash function** takes a key and transforms it into an index in the underlying array where the value should be stored. Ideally, the hash function should return a unique index for each key. However, since the number of possible keys is often much larger than the array size, there will inevitably be cases where multiple keys map to the same index. This is called a **collision**.

There are several techniques for handling collisions:

1. **Chaining**:
   o In chaining, each slot in the hash table holds a **linked list** (or another collection) of key-value pairs that map to the same index. When a collision occurs, the new key-value pair is added to the linked list at that index.
   o **Advantages**: Simple to implement; no need for resizing the hash table.
   o **Disadvantages**: Performance degrades when many collisions occur at a particular index, leading to longer linked lists.

Example of chaining:

python

```python
class HashTable:
    def __init__(self, size):
        self.size = size
        self.table = [[] for _ in range(size)]

    def hash_function(self, key):
        return hash(key) % self.size

    def insert(self, key, value):
        index = self.hash_function(key)
        # Check if key already exists in the list
        for i, (k, v) in enumerate(self.table[index]):
            if k == key:
                self.table[index][i] = (key, value)  # Update the value
                return
        self.table[index].append((key, value))  # Insert new key-value pair

    def get(self, key):
        index = self.hash_function(key)
        for k, v in self.table[index]:
```

```
    if k == key:

        return v

    return None  # Key not found


# Example usage
ht = HashTable(10)
ht.insert("apple", 100)
ht.insert("banana", 200)
print(ht.get("apple"))  # Output: 100
print(ht.get("banana"))  # Output: 200
```

2. **Open Addressing**:

   o In open addressing, when a collision occurs, the algorithm searches for the next available slot (or "probe") in the table. There are different strategies for finding the next available slot, such as **linear probing, quadratic probing**, or **double hashing**.

   o **Advantages**: Avoids the overhead of linked lists.

   o **Disadvantages**: Can result in clustering (groups of consecutive elements) and requires the table to be resized as it gets fuller.

Example of linear probing:

python

```python
class HashTable:
    def __init__(self, size):
        self.size = size
        self.table = [None] * size

    def hash_function(self, key):
        return hash(key) % self.size

    def insert(self, key, value):
        index = self.hash_function(key)
        # Linear probing: check subsequent slots for empty ones
        while self.table[index] is not None:
            if self.table[index][0] == key:
                self.table[index] = (key, value)  # Update value
                return
            index = (index + 1) % self.size  # Move to next slot
        self.table[index] = (key, value)

    def get(self, key):
        index = self.hash_function(key)
        while self.table[index] is not None:
            if self.table[index][0] == key:
                return self.table[index][1]
            index = (index + 1) % self.size
```

```
    return None  # Key not found
```

```
# Example usage
ht = HashTable(10)
ht.insert("apple", 100)
ht.insert("banana", 200)
print(ht.get("apple"))  # Output: 100
print(ht.get("banana"))  # Output: 200
```

Applications of Hash Tables

Hash tables are incredibly versatile and have many practical applications, especially in areas where fast lookups and unique key-value pair mappings are crucial. Here are some common use cases:

1. **Caching**:
   - Hash tables are used in caching systems to store previously computed values so that subsequent requests can be answered faster. In this case, the **key** is typically a request (e.g., a database query, image URL), and the **value** is the cached result (e.g., database response, image).

   Example: A web server might use a hash table to cache the results of expensive database queries. If the query is requested again, it can be retrieved directly from the cache, reducing the need to re-run the query.

2. **Indexing**:
   o Hash tables are used in indexing data, such as in search engines or databases. In these systems, a key (such as a word or document ID) is mapped to a value (such as the location of the document or the frequency of the word). This allows fast searches.

   Example: In a search engine, terms entered by the user can be hashed and used to find the relevant documents in an index very quickly.

3. **Database Lookups**:
   o Hash tables are often used in databases to provide fast retrieval of records based on unique keys (e.g., retrieving a user's profile based on their user ID). They allow databases to efficiently locate and return records without having to scan through entire datasets.

4. **Associative Arrays**:
   o In many programming languages, hash tables are the underlying structure behind **dictionaries** (Python) or **maps** (Java). These structures allow

developers to map keys to values in a way that ensures efficient lookups.

Example: A Python dict or Java HashMap is typically implemented using a hash table.

Hash tables are one of the most important and efficient data structures in computer science, providing quick access to data with their **constant time complexity** for insertion, deletion, and lookup operations. While the design of a good hash table involves careful consideration of hash functions and collision-handling strategies, the payoff is significant in terms of performance. Whether you're caching data, indexing information, or implementing key-value pair lookups in a database, understanding how hash tables work is fundamental to writing efficient algorithms and solving problems in real-world applications.

CHAPTER 8: TREES: ORGANIZING DATA HIERARCHICALLY

What Are Trees, and How Are They Structured?

A **tree** is a fundamental data structure that represents data in a hierarchical manner, much like a family tree or an organizational chart. Unlike linear data structures like arrays or linked lists, trees organize data in a branching structure where each item (node) can have multiple child nodes. This hierarchical structure makes trees especially useful for representing relationships between data points, where each node can have one or more descendants but only one parent (except for the root node).

A tree consists of the following components:

- **Node**: A single element in the tree that contains both data and references (links) to its children.
- **Root**: The topmost node in the tree, from which all other nodes descend.
- **Parent**: A node that has one or more child nodes.
- **Child**: A node that descends from another node (its parent).
- **Leaf**: A node with no children, representing the end of a branch.
- **Edge**: A link or reference between two nodes, connecting a parent to its child.

Trees are often used to model relationships where hierarchy is important, such as organizational charts, family trees, or directory structures in file systems.

Types of Trees

Trees come in various forms, each with different properties and use cases. Here are some of the most commonly used types of trees:

1. **Binary Tree:**

    o A **binary tree** is a tree where each node has at most **two children**, commonly referred to as the **left** and **right** children. This is the most basic form of a tree and serves as the foundation for many other types of trees.

    o **Example**: A binary tree used to store values can organize them in a structured way, allowing for efficient searches and insertions.

2. **Binary Search Tree (BST):**

    o A **binary search tree** is a binary tree with an additional property: for each node, all nodes in the **left subtree** have smaller values, and all nodes in the **right subtree** have larger values. This property allows for efficient searching, insertion, and deletion operations in **O(log n)** time for balanced trees.

    o **Example**: In a BST, if you want to find a specific number, you start at the root and decide whether to go left or right depending on whether the value you're looking for is smaller or larger than the current node.

Example of a Binary Search Tree:

plaintext

```
    50
   /  \
  30   70
 / \  / \
20 40 60  80
```

In the above tree, 50 is the root, 30 and 70 are its children, and so on. Notice how the left subtree of 50 contains only values less than 50, and the right subtree contains only values greater than 50.

3. **AVL Tree**:

   o   An **AVL tree** is a self-balancing binary search tree, where the difference in height between the left and right subtrees of any node is at most 1. This balancing ensures that operations like search, insert, and delete maintain a logarithmic time complexity, even in the worst case.

4. **Red-Black Tree**:

   o   A **red-black tree** is another type of self-balancing binary search tree. Each node in the tree has an extra bit for determining its color (red or black), and the tree maintains balancing rules based on these colors. This ensures that the tree remains balanced and operations like insertion, deletion, and search are efficient.

5. **Trie (Prefix Tree)**:
   - A **Trie** is a tree used for storing strings in a way that facilitates quick lookup of keys (strings). Each path down the tree represents a prefix of the key. Tries are commonly used in applications like autocomplete and spell checking.

6. **Heap**:
   - A **heap** is a binary tree-based structure that satisfies the **heap property**: in a **max-heap**, the value of each parent node is greater than or equal to the values of its children, while in a **min-heap**, the value of each parent node is smaller than or equal to the values of its children. Heaps are often used to implement priority queues.

Applications of Trees

Trees are widely used across many areas of computer science and software development, particularly in applications that require hierarchical organization or efficient searching. Some of the most notable use cases include:

1. **File Systems**:
   - File systems are a common example of a tree structure. Directories and files are organized hierarchically, with a root directory containing subdirectories and files. The organization of files

into folders and subfolders is modeled as a tree, where each directory can have multiple children (subdirectories and files).

Example: The file structure in Unix or Windows operating systems can be thought of as a tree structure:

plaintext

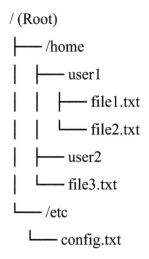

```
/ (Root)
├── /home
│   ├── user1
│   │   ├── file1.txt
│   │   └── file2.txt
│   ├── user2
│   └── file3.txt
└── /etc
    └── config.txt
```

2. **Decision Trees**:
   o Decision trees are used in machine learning to make decisions based on input data. Each node in a decision tree represents a decision based on a feature of the data, and the edges represent the outcome of that decision. Decision trees are

particularly useful for classification tasks, where the goal is to classify data into categories.

Example: In a decision tree for classifying whether an animal is a mammal or not, the decision nodes could be based on features like "Does it have fur?" and "Does it lay eggs?" The branches would lead to "Yes" or "No" outcomes, and the leaf nodes would represent the final classification.

3. **Expression Trees**:

   o An **expression tree** is a binary tree used to represent mathematical expressions. Internal nodes represent operators, and leaf nodes represent operands (such as numbers or variables). These trees are useful for evaluating expressions, parsing expressions, and compiling languages.

Example: The expression $((3 + 2) * (5 - 1))$ can be represented as:

plaintext

```
    *
   / \
  +   -
 / \ / \
```

3 25 1

4. **Routing Tables**:

   o Routing tables in networking use trees to efficiently store and look up routing paths. Each node in the tree represents a network, and the edges represent the routing paths to reach other networks.

   Example: In an IP routing table, a tree-like structure can be used to efficiently route packets from one network to another by checking each node (network) and deciding the best path to take based on destination.

Traversals: How to Visit All Nodes in a Tree

One of the fundamental operations on trees is **traversal**, which involves visiting each node in the tree in a specific order. There are several ways to traverse a tree, each with its own use case:

1. **In-order Traversal** (LNR):

   o In **in-order traversal**, you visit the left subtree, then the current node, and finally the right subtree. For binary search trees, in-order traversal visits nodes in ascending order.

Algorithm:

   o Traverse left subtree

- o Visit the current node
- o Traverse right subtree

Example:

python

```
def in_order_traversal(node):
    if node:
        in_order_traversal(node.left)
        print(node.value)
        in_order_traversal(node.right)
```

2. **Pre-order Traversal** (NLR):
   - o In **pre-order traversal**, you visit the current node first, then traverse the left subtree, and finally the right subtree. This is useful for creating a copy of a tree or evaluating expressions.

Algorithm:

- o Visit the current node
- o Traverse left subtree
- o Traverse right subtree

Example:

python

```python
def pre_order_traversal(node):
    if node:
        print(node.value)
        pre_order_traversal(node.left)
        pre_order_traversal(node.right)
```

3. **Post-order Traversal** (LRN):

   o In **post-order traversal**, you first traverse the left subtree, then the right subtree, and finally visit the current node. This is useful for deleting nodes in a tree or evaluating postfix expressions.

   Algorithm:

   o Traverse left subtree

   o Traverse right subtree

   o Visit the current node

   Example:

   python

```python
def post_order_traversal(node):
    if node:
        post_order_traversal(node.left)
        post_order_traversal(node.right)
```

```
print(node.value)
```

Trees are an essential and versatile data structure used to represent hierarchical relationships between elements. From file systems to machine learning algorithms, trees play a crucial role in organizing data efficiently. Understanding the different types of trees (binary trees, binary search trees, AVL trees, etc.) and their applications is fundamental to solving complex problems in computer science and software engineering. By mastering tree traversal techniques and leveraging the appropriate tree structure for a given problem, you can build efficient algorithms that work well with hierarchical data.

CHAPTER 9: BALANCED TREES AND HEAPS

Understanding AVL and Red-Black Trees

In computer science, the need for maintaining efficient tree operations (such as searching, inserting, and deleting) is crucial for performance, especially in large datasets. Balanced trees are specifically designed to keep the tree structure balanced, ensuring that the operations on the tree remain efficient, even in the worst-case scenario. Let's explore two of the most commonly used types of balanced trees: **AVL trees** and **Red-Black trees**.

1. AVL Trees

An **AVL tree** (named after its inventors Adelson-Velsky and Landis) is a self-balancing **binary search tree** where the difference in heights between the left and right subtrees of any node is at most **1**. This property ensures that the tree remains balanced, preventing it from degenerating into a linked list, which would lead to inefficient operations.

- **Balancing Factor**: For each node, the **balance factor** is calculated as the difference in height between the left and right subtrees. The balance factor must be -1, 0, or 1 for the tree to be considered balanced.

- **Rebalancing**: If a node's balance factor becomes less than -1 or greater than 1 after an insertion or deletion, the tree undergoes **rotations** (left or right rotations) to restore balance.

Rotations in AVL Trees:

1. **Single Right Rotation (LL Rotation)**:
   - Used when a left-heavy subtree needs balancing.
   - The left child becomes the new root of the subtree.

2. **Single Left Rotation (RR Rotation)**:
   - Used when a right-heavy subtree needs balancing.
   - The right child becomes the new root of the subtree.

3. **Left-Right Rotation (LR Rotation)**:
   - A combination of a left rotation followed by a right rotation, used when the left child's right subtree is heavy.

4. **Right-Left Rotation (RL Rotation)**:
   - A combination of a right rotation followed by a left rotation, used when the right child's left subtree is heavy.

Example of AVL Tree:

Inserting values into an AVL tree results in balancing the tree through rotations when necessary.

plaintext

Before Insertion (Unbalanced):
```
30
/
20
/
```

10

After Insertion (Balanced through rotation):

```
  20
 / \
10  30
```

2. Red-Black Trees

A **Red-Black Tree** is another type of self-balancing binary search tree, but it uses **coloring** to enforce balance. Each node in the tree is either **red** or **black**, and the tree follows a set of rules that maintain balance.

Properties of Red-Black Trees:

1. **Root**: The root is always black.
2. **Red Nodes**: Red nodes cannot have red children (i.e., no two red nodes can be adjacent).
3. **Black Height**: Every path from a node to its descendant leaves must have the same number of black nodes.
4. **New Insertions**: New nodes are always inserted as **red**. After insertion, the tree may need to be restructured (via rotations) and recolored to maintain the Red-Black properties.

Rotations in Red-Black Trees:

Similar to AVL trees, **rotations** are used to maintain the balance of the tree after insertion or deletion operations.

- **Left Rotation**: A right child becomes the new parent.
- **Right Rotation**: A left child becomes the new parent.

Example of Red-Black Tree Properties:

Inserting values into a Red-Black Tree requires enforcing the above properties. After insertion, the tree may need to be recolored and rotated to maintain balance.

3. Binary Heaps: Min-Heaps and Max-Heaps

A **binary heap** is a **complete binary tree** that satisfies the **heap property**. There are two types of heaps:

- **Min-Heap**: In a min-heap, the value of the parent node is always **less than or equal to** the values of its children. This makes the smallest element in the heap always at the root.
- **Max-Heap**: In a max-heap, the value of the parent node is always **greater than or equal to** the values of its children. This makes the largest element in the heap always at the root.

Heap Operations:

1. **Insert**: Insertion in a binary heap involves adding a new element at the bottom of the tree and then "bubbling up" to restore the heap property.

2. **Extract-Min/Extract-Max**: To remove the root (the smallest element in a min-heap or the largest element in a max-heap), we replace the root with the last element and then "heapify down" to restore the heap property.

3. **Heapify**: The process of rearranging the tree to satisfy the heap property, either by "bubbling up" or "bubbling down" elements.

Example of Min-Heap:

plaintext

```
Min-Heap:
    10
   / \
  20   30
 / \
40  50


After extracting the min (10):
    20
   / \
  50   30
 /
```

40

In the min-heap above, the smallest element (10) is at the root. After extraction, the tree reorganizes to maintain the heap property.

4. Applications of Balanced Trees and Heaps

Balanced trees and heaps are used in a variety of real-world applications due to their efficiency in handling dynamic datasets:

- **Priority Queues**: Both AVL trees and Red-Black trees can be used to implement priority queues, where the highest (or lowest) priority element is always accessible. Heaps, particularly binary heaps, are commonly used to implement priority queues because of their efficient insertion and deletion operations.

  Example: A priority queue is used in **job scheduling** systems, where tasks are processed based on their priority.

- **Median Finding**: A common use of heaps is in **median finding** algorithms, where we can use two heaps (a max-heap and a min-heap) to efficiently maintain the median of a dynamic set of numbers.

  Example: In a streaming application where data is continuously arriving, maintaining the median of the dataset in real-time can be done efficiently by using two heaps.

- **Sorting**: Heaps are also used in **heap sort**, a comparison-based sorting algorithm. While not as commonly used as other sorting algorithms like QuickSort or MergeSort, it has the advantage of being in-place and having a worst-case time complexity of O(n log n).

5. Maintaining Balance and Efficiency in Tree Structures

The key benefit of balanced trees (like AVL and Red-Black trees) and heaps is that they provide efficient solutions for operations like **insertion**, **deletion**, and **searching** in dynamic datasets. By ensuring that the trees remain balanced after every operation, these data structures guarantee that the time complexity remains **logarithmic** (O(log n)), which is crucial for performance when dealing with large datasets.

To maintain efficiency:

- **AVL trees** enforce stricter balancing through rotations after each insertion and deletion, ensuring that the height difference between subtrees never exceeds 1.
- **Red-Black trees** use a more relaxed balancing method based on colors, but they still guarantee that operations will take O(log n) time, making them a popular choice for applications that require frequent insertions and deletions.
- **Heaps** provide an efficient way to manage dynamic sets of data where the order of priority matters, ensuring that the

most important element can always be accessed in constant time, with insertion and deletion operations taking logarithmic time.

Balanced trees and heaps are powerful data structures that ensure high performance for various operations, from searching and insertion to deletion and sorting. AVL and Red-Black trees provide self-balancing solutions for maintaining efficient search operations in binary search trees, while binary heaps are highly effective for priority queue management and median finding. Understanding these structures, along with their applications and internal balancing mechanisms, is essential for designing efficient algorithms that handle dynamic data.

CHAPTER 10: GRAPHS: CONNECTING THE DOTS

Graphs are one of the most versatile and fundamental data structures in computer science, used to represent relationships or connections between objects. In this chapter, we'll explore the structure of graphs, their types, and how they're applied to solve complex real-world problems. By the end of the chapter, you'll have a solid understanding of how graphs are represented, traversed, and utilized in a variety of domains.

1. What Are Graphs, and Where Are They Used?

A **graph** is a collection of **nodes** (also called **vertices**) and **edges** (also called **arcs**) that connect pairs of nodes. Graphs are used to model relationships or connections between objects. Each node represents an entity, and each edge represents a connection between two entities.

Graphs can be found in numerous real-world applications, including:

- **Social Networks**: Nodes represent individuals, and edges represent friendships, followers, or interactions. Graphs help model how users are connected, which can be used for recommendations or identifying communities.
- **Transportation Systems**: In a map, cities or stations are represented as nodes, and the roads or train tracks between them are edges. Graph algorithms can help find the shortest route or determine connectivity.

- **Web Pages and Links**: In the context of the internet, web pages are nodes, and hyperlinks between them are edges. Search engines like Google use graph traversal techniques to index and rank pages.

- **Recommendation Systems**: By modeling user-product relationships as a graph, algorithms can recommend products based on user behavior, preferences, and similarities to other users.

Graphs are especially useful in representing problems where relationships and connectivity are key, such as in routing, networking, clustering, and even game theory.

2. Types of Graphs

There are several ways in which graphs can be classified, depending on the nature of their edges and how they connect nodes.

a. Directed vs. Undirected Graphs

- **Directed Graph (Digraph)**: In a directed graph, each edge has a direction, going from one node to another. This means the edges are ordered, and the connection is one-way. For example, in a **social network** on Twitter, the edges represent "follows," and they are directed since if **A follows B**, it doesn't mean **B follows A**.

- **Undirected Graph**: In an undirected graph, the edges have no direction, meaning the connection between nodes is bidirectional. A classic example is a **Facebook** friendship where, if **A is friends with B**, then **B is also friends with A**.

b. Weighted vs. Unweighted Graphs

- **Weighted Graph**: In a weighted graph, each edge has an associated value or weight that represents the cost, distance, or any other metric that quantifies the connection between nodes. For example, in a **transportation system** graph, the weight of an edge could represent the travel time between two cities.

- **Unweighted Graph**: An unweighted graph doesn't have any weights or costs associated with its edges. The connections between nodes are simply binary: there is a connection or there isn't. This type of graph can be used in problems where only the existence of a connection matters, not its cost or distance (e.g., social networks).

Examples:

- **Directed Weighted Graph**: A transportation map with one-way streets, where the edges are streets, and the weights represent distances or travel time.
- **Undirected Unweighted Graph**: A simple social network, where the nodes are people and the edges represent friendships.

3. Graph Representations: Adjacency Matrix and List

There are multiple ways to represent graphs in memory. Two of the most common methods are the **adjacency matrix** and the **adjacency list**. The choice of representation affects both the space and time complexity of graph operations.

a. Adjacency Matrix

An **adjacency matrix** is a 2D array (a square matrix) used to represent a graph. Each row and column represents a node in the graph, and the cell at position $(i,j)(i, j)(i,j)$ indicates whether there is an edge between node iii and node jjj.

- **For undirected graphs**, the matrix is symmetric since if there's an edge from iii to jjj, there's also an edge from jjj to iii.
- **For directed graphs**, the matrix is not necessarily symmetric.

In the case of **weighted graphs**, the matrix stores the weight of the edge in place of a binary value (1 or 0).

Example: A simple undirected graph with 3 nodes (A, B, C) and edges A-B and B-C would be represented by the following adjacency matrix:

A B C

A B C

A 0 1 0

B 1 0 1

C 0 1 0

In this matrix:

- 1 at position (A,B)(A, B)(A,B) and (B,A)(B, A)(B,A) indicates an edge between A and B.
- 1 at position (B,C)(B, C)(B,C) and (C,B)(C, B)(C,B) indicates an edge between B and C.
- 0 indicates no direct edge between those nodes.

b. Adjacency List

An **adjacency list** is an array (or a list) of lists. Each element of the array corresponds to a node, and the list at that position contains all the neighbors of that node. This representation is more space-efficient than an adjacency matrix for sparse graphs (graphs with few edges relative to the number of nodes).

Example: Using the same graph (A-B, B-C):

Node Neighbors

A   B

Node Neighbors

B   A, C

C   B

In this example, node A has a connection to node B, node B has connections to nodes A and C, and node C has a connection to node B.

4. Real-World Examples of Graphs

Graphs are used in a wide array of domains, often to model complex systems with multiple interconnected elements.

a. Social Networks

In social media platforms like Facebook or LinkedIn, users are represented as nodes, and their relationships (friendships, followers, etc.) are represented as edges. Graph algorithms are used to analyze the connections and recommend friends, suggest groups, or identify communities.

For example:

- **Friend Recommendations**: By analyzing the graph structure, a social media platform can recommend friends to a user based on mutual connections.

- **Community Detection**: Algorithms can detect clusters or communities within the graph, identifying groups of users who are more interconnected.

b. Transportation Systems

Graphs are used in transportation networks, where locations (e.g., cities, stations) are nodes, and routes (e.g., roads, train tracks) are edges. Graph algorithms help to find the **shortest path**, **optimal route**, or **network flow**.

For example:

- **Shortest Path Algorithm**: Dijkstra's algorithm can find the shortest route between two cities in a road network.
- **Traveling Salesman Problem (TSP)**: A famous optimization problem where a salesman must visit several cities, minimizing travel distance or cost, which can be modeled as a graph.

c. Web Page Link Structure

The World Wide Web is another real-world example where the web pages are nodes and hyperlinks between them are edges. Algorithms like **PageRank** (used by Google) are applied to rank web pages based on their importance or relevance, which is derived from the structure of the web graph.

For example:

- **Web Crawling**: Crawlers explore web pages by following links between them, using graph traversal techniques like **breadth-first search (BFS)** or **depth-first search (DFS)**.
- **Link Prediction**: Algorithms can predict potential new links between pages based on the existing graph structure.

Graphs provide a powerful abstraction for modeling relationships and solving complex problems in diverse areas like social networks, transportation, and the web. Understanding the different types of graphs, their representations, and how to apply graph algorithms is essential for tackling problems involving connected data. In this chapter, we've covered the fundamentals of graphs, from their structure to common real-world applications. In the next chapters, we'll dive deeper into graph traversal algorithms and advanced topics, helping you harness the full potential of graphs in your algorithms.

CHAPTER 11: DYNAMIC GRAPHS AND ADVANCED GRAPH DATA STRUCTURES

In this chapter, we will dive into more advanced graph algorithms and data structures. These concepts extend the basic graph theory we discussed earlier and are essential for solving complex problems in dynamic systems such as network optimization, routing, and logistics. Whether you're working on transportation networks, logistics, or analyzing large-scale data, understanding these advanced graph techniques will help you address real-world challenges efficiently.

1. Spanning Trees: Prim's and Kruskal's Algorithms

A **spanning tree** of a connected graph is a subset of the graph's edges that connects all the vertices together without forming any cycles. In other words, a spanning tree includes all the vertices of the graph, but with the minimum number of edges possible to maintain connectivity. This concept is fundamental in network design, where you want to minimize the cost or length of connections while ensuring every point in the network is accessible.

Two widely-used algorithms for finding a minimum spanning tree (MST) are **Prim's Algorithm** and **Kruskal's Algorithm**. Both algorithms have their specific use cases and efficiency considerations.

a. Prim's Algorithm

Prim's algorithm builds the MST incrementally, starting from an arbitrary node and adding the minimum-weight edge that connects a vertex in the tree to a vertex outside the tree. This process continues until all vertices are included in the tree.

- **Key Idea**: Greedily select the minimum weight edge that expands the tree.
- **Time Complexity**: $O(E\log V)O(E \log V)O(ElogV)$, where EEE is the number of edges and VVV is the number of vertices, assuming a priority queue is used.
- **Use Case**: Best used when the graph is dense, i.e., it has many edges.

b. Kruskal's Algorithm

Kruskal's algorithm, on the other hand, works by sorting all the edges in the graph in increasing order of weight and then adding edges one by one to the MST, ensuring that no cycles are formed. Kruskal's algorithm uses a **disjoint-set (union-find)** data structure to efficiently check whether adding an edge creates a cycle.

- **Key Idea**: Sort all edges, then add the shortest edge that doesn't create a cycle.
- **Time Complexity**: $O(E\log E)O(E \log E)O(ElogE)$, where EEE is the number of edges.
- **Use Case**: Best used when the graph is sparse, i.e., it has relatively few edges.

Example:

Imagine a logistics company wants to minimize the cost of laying roads between cities to create a delivery network. Using a minimum spanning tree algorithm, they can find the set of roads that connect all cities with the least cost while avoiding redundant paths.

2. Shortest Path Problems: Dijkstra's and Bellman-Ford Algorithms

The **shortest path problem** is one of the most fundamental problems in graph theory and is concerned with finding the shortest path between two nodes in a weighted graph. This problem arises in numerous real-world applications, such as GPS navigation systems, network routing protocols, and traffic management.

a. Dijkstra's Algorithm

Dijkstra's algorithm is a **greedy** algorithm that finds the shortest path from a source node to all other nodes in a graph. It works by visiting nodes in increasing order of distance from the source, updating the shortest known distance to each node along the way.

- **Key Idea**: Use a priority queue to always expand the least-cost path.
- **Time Complexity**: $O(E \log V)$ $O(E \log V)$ $O(E \log V)$, where E is the number of edges and V is the number of vertices, assuming a priority queue is used.

- **Limitation**: Dijkstra's algorithm only works for graphs with non-negative edge weights.

b. Bellman-Ford Algorithm

The Bellman-Ford algorithm is another algorithm to find the shortest path from a single source to all other vertices in a weighted graph. Unlike Dijkstra, Bellman-Ford can handle graphs with **negative edge weights** and can even detect negative weight cycles (which would imply an infinitely decreasing path).

- **Key Idea**: Relax all edges repeatedly to find the shortest path.
- **Time Complexity**: $O(VE)O(VE)O(VE)$, where VVV is the number of vertices and EEE is the number of edges.
- **Limitation**: Slower than Dijkstra's algorithm for graphs with positive weights, but more versatile due to its ability to handle negative weights.

Example:

In a routing system, where roads might have different travel times (some positive, others negative, such as detours or road closures), Bellman-Ford can help find the shortest path, even when a negative time cost is involved. Dijkstra's algorithm would be more efficient if all roads had positive time costs.

3. Network Flows and Connectivity

The concept of **network flow** is used to model the flow of resources through a network. A common problem in network flow is finding the **maximum flow** in a flow network, such as the maximum amount of data that can be transferred through a network of computers, or the maximum amount of goods that can be transported through a set of supply routes.

a. Ford-Fulkerson Algorithm

The **Ford-Fulkerson algorithm** is used to find the maximum flow in a flow network. The algorithm works by repeatedly finding augmenting paths (paths that increase the flow from the source to the sink) and increasing the flow along those paths.

- **Key Idea**: Use augmenting paths to increase flow until no more augmenting paths exist.
- **Time Complexity**: The complexity of Ford-Fulkerson depends on the number of augmenting paths found. The **Edmonds-Karp** implementation improves this to $O(VE2)O(VE^2)O(VE2)$.

b. Edmonds-Karp Algorithm

The **Edmonds-Karp algorithm** is an implementation of Ford-Fulkerson that uses **breadth-first search (BFS)** to find augmenting paths. This ensures that the algorithm finds the shortest augmenting paths first, improving the overall efficiency.

- **Time Complexity**: O(VE2)O(VE^2)O(VE2), where VVV is the number of vertices and EEE is the number of edges.

Real-Life Applications:

- **Supply Chains**: In logistics, network flow algorithms can help optimize transportation systems by calculating the maximum number of goods that can be delivered from a warehouse to multiple destinations, given the capacity limits of different routes.
- **Telecommunication Networks**: Network flow algorithms are used to maximize data throughput in communication networks by determining the maximum flow of information that can be sent from one node to another.

4. Real-Life Applications: Routing Algorithms and Logistics

Routing and logistics are areas where graph algorithms are critical in solving practical problems. Whether it's determining the fastest route, managing resource distribution, or optimizing transport networks, graph theory provides the foundation for these problems.

a. Shortest Path in Logistics

In logistics, companies often need to determine the **shortest delivery route** for trucks to travel between various warehouses and distribution centers. Dijkstra's algorithm is typically used here to calculate the fastest route from the starting warehouse to any other location in the system.

b. Traffic Routing

In a **traffic management system**, graphs are used to represent roads as edges and intersections as nodes. Algorithms like Dijkstra's or A* are used to find the shortest route from a source (such as a driver's current location) to a destination (such as their home or office). This can be applied to real-time traffic data to help avoid congestion or accidents.

c. Communication Networks

Graphs are also used in **telecommunication networks** to route data packets between different servers and devices. The goal is to maximize the flow of data while minimizing delays. Network flow algorithms are crucial for optimizing data transmission and ensuring the network can handle large volumes of traffic efficiently.

d. Airline Routing

In the **airline industry**, the routes between airports form a graph where each airport is a node, and each flight between airports is an edge. Optimizing flight paths to minimize costs and delays is a classical example of applying graph theory, where algorithms like Dijkstra's or the Bellman-Ford algorithm can be used to find the most efficient routes.

In this chapter, we explored advanced graph algorithms that help solve complex problems in real-world systems. From **spanning trees** and **shortest path algorithms** to **network flow** and **routing**, these algorithms are at the core of many optimization problems, including logistics, transportation, and communication networks. Understanding these algorithms equips you with the tools needed to design efficient solutions to dynamic and interconnected systems.

Next, we will move into more practical applications of graph algorithms and explore how to implement them efficiently in Python for real-world use cases.

CHAPTER 12: DIVIDE AND CONQUER

The **Divide and Conquer** paradigm is a foundational approach in algorithm design that solves problems by breaking them into smaller subproblems, solving those subproblems independently, and then combining their solutions to solve the original problem. It is particularly effective for problems that can be divided into similar smaller instances of themselves, a concept known as **self-similarity**.

1. Breaking Problems Into Smaller Parts

The core idea of divide and conquer involves three main steps:

1. **Divide**:
    - Split the original problem into smaller subproblems.
    - These subproblems should ideally be of the same type as the original problem and significantly smaller in size.

2. **Conquer**:
    - Solve each subproblem recursively. If the subproblem size is small enough, solve it directly (this is the **base case** of the recursion).

3. **Combine**:

○ Combine the solutions of the subproblems to form the solution to the original problem.

Example: Consider sorting an array:

- **Divide**: Split the array into two halves.
- **Conquer**: Sort each half recursively.
- **Combine**: Merge the sorted halves into a single sorted array.

2. Classic Algorithms

Several well-known algorithms are based on the divide and conquer approach. Two of the most prominent examples are **merge sort** and **quicksort**, which are used for sorting arrays.

a. Merge Sort

Merge sort is a sorting algorithm that divides the array into halves, recursively sorts each half, and then merges the two sorted halves.

Algorithm:

1. Divide the array into two halves.
2. Conquer: Recursively sort each half.
3. Combine: Merge the two sorted halves.

Time Complexity: $O(n\log n)$ for all cases (best, average, worst).

Example in Python:

python

```python
def merge_sort(arr):
    if len(arr) > 1:
        mid = len(arr) // 2
        left_half = arr[:mid]
        right_half = arr[mid:]

        # Recursively sort both halves
        merge_sort(left_half)
        merge_sort(right_half)

        # Merge the sorted halves
        i = j = k = 0
        while i < len(left_half) and j < len(right_half):
            if left_half[i] < right_half[j]:
                arr[k] = left_half[i]
                i += 1
            else:
                arr[k] = right_half[j]
                j += 1
            k += 1

        while i < len(left_half):
```

```
arr[k] = left_half[i]
i += 1
k += 1

while j < len(right_half):
    arr[k] = right_half[j]
    j += 1
    k += 1
```

b. Quicksort

Quicksort is a sorting algorithm that selects a "pivot" element, partitions the array into elements less than and greater than the pivot, and then recursively sorts the partitions.

Algorithm:

1. Choose a pivot element (commonly the first or last element, or chosen randomly).
2. Partition the array so that all elements less than the pivot come before it and all elements greater come after it.
3. Recursively sort the left and right partitions.

Time Complexity:

- Best and average case: $O(nlogn)O(n \log n)O(nlogn)$.
- Worst case: $O(n2)O(n^2)O(n2)$ (when the pivot is poorly chosen).

Example in Python:

python

```
def quicksort(arr):
    if len(arr) <= 1:
        return arr
    pivot = arr[0]
    less_than_pivot = [x for x in arr[1:] if x <= pivot]
    greater_than_pivot = [x for x in arr[1:] if x > pivot]
    return    quicksort(less_than_pivot)    +    [pivot]    +
quicksort(greater_than_pivot)
```

3. Applications

Divide and conquer is not limited to sorting algorithms. It has applications in a variety of fields and problems, including:

a. Large-Scale Data Analysis

Divide and conquer is particularly useful in processing large datasets that cannot fit into memory all at once. By dividing the data into smaller chunks, each chunk can be processed independently, and the results can be combined.

- **Example**: Distributed systems like **MapReduce** use divide and conquer principles to split datasets across multiple machines, process each piece, and then aggregate the results.

b. Matrix Multiplication

Divide and conquer is used in **Strassen's algorithm** for matrix multiplication, which is more efficient than the naive $O(n3)O(n^3)O(n3)$ approach. It divides matrices into submatrices, performs recursive multiplications, and combines the results.

Strassen's Algorithm Time Complexity: $O(nlog⚹27)≈O(n2.81)O(n^{\log_2 7}) \approx O(n^{2.81})O(nlog27)≈O(n2.81)$.

c. Computational Geometry

Divide and conquer is used in geometric algorithms, such as:

- **Finding the closest pair of points** in a 2D space $(O(nlog⚹n)O(n \log n)O(nlogn))$.
- **Convex hull algorithms** for identifying the smallest convex polygon enclosing a set of points.

4. Advantages and Pitfalls of the Approach

Advantages

1. **Efficiency**:
   - Divide and conquer often reduces the time complexity of problems compared to brute force methods.
   - It is particularly effective for problems with a natural recursive structure.

2. **Parallelism**:

   o Subproblems are independent of each other, making divide and conquer well-suited for parallel computing.

3. **Simplicity**:

   o Many complex problems can be broken into simpler subproblems, making the algorithm easier to design and understand.

Pitfalls

1. **Overhead**:

   o Recursion can introduce overhead due to repeated function calls and stack usage.

   o Combining results may also add extra computational cost.

2. **Base Case Complexity**:

   o If the base case isn't well-defined or simple to solve, the algorithm may become inefficient.

3. **Dependency on Input**:

   o For some algorithms (e.g., quicksort), the performance heavily depends on the input (e.g., choice of pivot).

Example of a Pitfall in Quicksort:

If the pivot is always chosen as the first or last element, and the array is already sorted, quicksort degrades to $O(n2)O(n^2)O(n2)$.

The **divide and conquer** paradigm is a powerful tool in algorithm design, providing a structured approach to breaking down complex problems into manageable subproblems. Algorithms like **merge sort** and **quicksort** demonstrate the elegance and efficiency of this technique, while applications in large-scale data processing and computational geometry show its versatility.

Understanding the trade-offs between the advantages and pitfalls of divide and conquer helps you decide when to use this approach and how to optimize its implementation. In the next chapter, we'll explore another core algorithmic paradigm: **Dynamic Programming**, which is especially useful for solving problems with overlapping subproblems and optimal substructure.

CHAPTER 13: BACKTRACKING

Backtracking is a powerful algorithmic technique used to solve problems where the solution space is large, and we need to explore all possible solutions systematically while adhering to constraints. It is particularly useful for solving problems that involve combinatorial searches, where we build a solution incrementally and discard partial solutions as soon as they are determined to be invalid. Backtracking is essentially a **depth-first search** that explores all potential solutions, backtracking when it finds that a given path doesn't lead to a valid solution.

1. Exploring All Possibilities Systematically

Backtracking is often described as **"trial and error with pruning"**. The basic idea is to try out different possibilities in a structured way, **"backtrack"** when we hit an invalid or undesirable state, and proceed to explore other options. It's a general algorithm for solving problems with constraints, where:

1. We incrementally build a solution.
2. Whenever a partial solution violates a constraint, we backtrack (i.e., discard the current path and try a new one).

3. If a solution is found, we continue; otherwise, we discard the current solution and try another possibility.

The key feature of backtracking is that it allows us to **prune** the search tree and avoid exploring solutions that we know are invalid, thus reducing the search space.

2. Examples of Backtracking Problems

a. N-Queens Problem

The N-Queens problem is a classic backtracking problem in which we must place N queens on an N×N chessboard in such a way that no two queens threaten each other. A queen can attack another queen if they share the same row, column, or diagonal.

Steps:

- Start placing queens one by one in different columns.
- For each column, try all possible rows for placing a queen.
- When placing a queen in a row results in a conflict with the already placed queens (either in the same row, column, or diagonal), backtrack and try the next possibility.

Solution in Python:

python

```python
def is_safe(board, row, col, N):
```

```python
    for i in range(col):
        if board[row][i] == 1:
            return False
    for i, j in zip(range(row, -1, -1), range(col, -1, -1)):
        if board[i][j] == 1:
            return False
    for i, j in zip(range(row, N), range(col, -1, -1)):
        if board[i][j] == 1:
            return False
    return True


def solve_nqueens(board, col, N):
    if col >= N:
        return True

    for i in range(N):
        if is_safe(board, i, col, N):
            board[i][col] = 1
            if solve_nqueens(board, col + 1, N):
                return True
            board[i][col] = 0

    return False


def print_board(board, N):
```

```
for row in board:
    print(" ".join(str(x) for x in row))


N = 4
board = [[0 for _ in range(N)] for _ in range(N)]
if solve_nqueens(board, 0, N):
    print_board(board, N)
else:
    print("Solution does not exist")
```

b. Sudoku Solver

The Sudoku puzzle is another classic problem that can be solved using backtracking. The task is to fill a 9×9 grid with digits (1–9) such that each row, each column, and each of the nine 3×3 subgrids contains all the digits from 1 to 9 without repetition.

Steps:

1. Pick an empty cell.
2. Try filling the cell with digits from 1 to 9.
3. Check if the current number violates any Sudoku constraints (row, column, or subgrid).
4. If it does, backtrack and try the next number.
5. Repeat until the entire board is filled.

Solution in Python:

python

```python
def is_valid(board, row, col, num):
    for i in range(9):
        if board[row][i] == num or board[i][col] == num:
            return False
    start_row, start_col = 3 * (row // 3), 3 * (col // 3)
    for i in range(start_row, start_row + 3):
        for j in range(start_col, start_col + 3):
            if board[i][j] == num:
                return False
    return True


def solve_sudoku(board):
    for row in range(9):
        for col in range(9):
            if board[row][col] == 0:
                for num in range(1, 10):
                    if is_valid(board, row, col, num):
                        board[row][col] = num
                        if solve_sudoku(board):
                            return True
                        board[row][col] = 0
                return False
    return True
```

```
def print_board(board):
    for row in board:
        print(" ".join(str(x) for x in row))


board = [
    [5, 3, 0, 0, 7, 0, 0, 0, 0],
    [6, 0, 0, 1, 9, 5, 0, 0, 0],
    [0, 9, 8, 0, 0, 0, 0, 6, 0],
    [8, 0, 0, 0, 6, 0, 0, 0, 3],
    [4, 0, 0, 8, 0, 3, 0, 0, 1],
    [7, 0, 0, 0, 2, 0, 0, 0, 6],
    [0, 6, 0, 0, 0, 0, 2, 8, 0],
    [0, 0, 0, 4, 1, 9, 0, 0, 5],
    [0, 0, 0, 0, 8, 0, 0, 7, 9]
]


if solve_sudoku(board):
    print_board(board)
else:
    print("No solution exists")
```

3. Real-World Applications: Constraint Satisfaction Problems

Backtracking is not limited to puzzles and games; it has real-world applications in solving **constraint satisfaction problems** (CSPs).

These problems involve finding solutions that satisfy a set of constraints, such as:

- **Sudoku** (as shown above)
- **Graph coloring**, where you assign colors to nodes such that no two adjacent nodes share the same color.
- **Job scheduling**, where you must allocate jobs to resources under constraints (e.g., minimizing overlap or making use of limited resources).
- **Crossword puzzles**, where you must fit words into a grid, following the rules of letter placement.

4. Performance Considerations and Pruning Techniques

While backtracking is effective, it can be inefficient for large problems due to its exhaustive search nature. To improve performance, various pruning techniques are used to eliminate invalid paths early:

a. Early Stopping

- Whenever we detect that a solution is invalid (either through constraint violations or other checks), we can stop searching down that path and backtrack immediately.

b. Heuristics

- In some problems, we can use heuristics to prioritize certain branches of the search tree, which can improve the chances of finding a solution faster.

**c. Forward Checking

- In problems like Sudoku, forward checking involves examining the potential consequences of each step, eliminating choices that would lead to dead ends sooner.

d. Constraint Propagation

- This is used in CSPs, where we propagate constraints across the system as we make choices, reducing the size of the search space and speeding up the solution process.

Backtracking is a versatile and powerful technique used to solve a wide range of combinatorial and constraint satisfaction problems. Whether solving puzzles like N-Queens or Sudoku, or tackling real-world problems such as job scheduling or resource allocation, backtracking provides a systematic way to explore all potential solutions while pruning invalid paths to save time. By understanding its structure and applying optimization techniques, you can significantly improve the efficiency of backtracking algorithms.

In the next chapter, we'll dive into **Dynamic Programming**, another essential algorithmic technique that builds solutions incrementally but differs from backtracking in its approach to overlapping subproblems.

CHAPTER 14: PARALLEL AND DISTRIBUTED ALGORITHMS

In the rapidly evolving world of computing, the sheer scale and complexity of modern problems require us to think beyond traditional sequential algorithms. **Parallel** and **distributed algorithms** are fundamental approaches that enable more efficient problem-solving by leveraging multiple processors or machines simultaneously. These techniques are increasingly vital in fields such as big data processing, cloud computing, machine learning, and artificial intelligence.

This chapter explores the theory and applications of parallel and distributed algorithms, starting with the basics of parallel computing and extending to more complex distributed systems. Understanding these concepts is essential for tackling large-scale computational challenges in today's world.

1. The Need for Parallel and Distributed Systems

Modern computational problems often involve vast amounts of data or complex computations that cannot be handled efficiently on a single processor. In these cases, using multiple processors or machines to work in parallel can drastically speed up the computation. Let's break down the differences:

- **Parallel computing** involves using multiple processors or cores within a single machine to divide and process tasks concurrently. This is particularly useful for problems that can be broken down into independent, smaller tasks.
- **Distributed computing** takes parallelism to the next level by using multiple machines, often geographically dispersed, to solve a problem collaboratively. This setup is beneficial for problems that need vast amounts of memory or computing power, like big data processing and cloud applications.

For instance, **Google** uses parallel and distributed systems for indexing the web and processing massive datasets using **MapReduce**, and **Amazon** relies on distributed algorithms for ensuring that their cloud services are highly available and fault-tolerant.

The advent of cloud computing and big data has pushed the boundaries of what can be accomplished using these approaches, making parallel and distributed algorithms essential for modern software development.

2. Parallel Algorithms: MapReduce and Divide-and-Conquer

Parallel algorithms break down a problem into smaller tasks that can be solved simultaneously by multiple processors or cores. A few popular approaches and algorithms in parallel computing include **MapReduce** and **Divide-and-Conquer** strategies.

a. MapReduce

MapReduce is a programming model popularized by Google for processing large-scale data in parallel across distributed systems. The process consists of two main steps:

- **Map**: The input data is divided into smaller chunks, and the map function is applied to each chunk. The map function processes the data in parallel, usually transforming the data into key-value pairs.
- **Reduce**: After the map phase, the intermediate data (key-value pairs) is shuffled and grouped by the key, and the reduce function is applied to aggregate or summarize the results.

This model is particularly useful for **big data** processing, such as sorting large datasets, counting word frequencies in text, or filtering large collections of data.

Example: Counting Word Frequency in a Large Dataset

1. **Map step**: Break the text into words, and output a key-value pair for each word (e.g., (word, 1)).
2. **Shuffle**: Group by key, resulting in a list of all occurrences of the same word.
3. **Reduce step**: For each word, sum the occurrences to get the total count.

python

```python
from collections import defaultdict

def map_step(data):
    result = defaultdict(int)
    for word in data.split():
        result[word] += 1
    return result

def reduce_step(mapped_data):
    total = defaultdict(int)
    for data in mapped_data:
```

```python
    for word, count in data.items():
        total[word] += count
    return total


data_chunks = ["hello world", "hello data", "data world"]
mapped = [map_step(chunk) for chunk in data_chunks]
result = reduce_step(mapped)


print(result)
```

b. Divide-and-Conquer

The divide-and-conquer approach is a classical algorithmic technique where a problem is recursively divided into smaller subproblems, which are solved independently and then combined to form the final solution. It is particularly effective for tasks that have overlapping subproblems, where the solution can be broken into smaller, independent parts.

Common algorithms that use divide-and-conquer include:

- **Merge Sort**
- **Quick Sort**
- **Matrix Multiplication**

Example: Merge Sort (Parallelized)

python

```python
def merge_sort(arr):
    if len(arr) <= 1:
        return arr
    mid = len(arr) // 2
    left = merge_sort(arr[:mid])
    right = merge_sort(arr[mid:])
    return merge(left, right)

def merge(left, right):
    result = []
    i = j = 0
    while i < len(left) and j < len(right):
        if left[i] < right[j]:
            result.append(left[i])
            i += 1
        else:
            result.append(right[j])
            j += 1
    result.extend(left[i:])
    result.extend(right[j:])
    return result
```

By dividing the array into two halves and recursively sorting each half in parallel, the merge sort algorithm can be parallelized effectively. In a distributed system, the tasks can be divided among multiple machines, speeding up the sorting process significantly.

3. *Distributed Systems: Consensus Algorithms and Fault Tolerance*

Distributed systems involve coordinating multiple machines to solve a problem or complete a task. Ensuring that these machines work together smoothly is crucial, especially in the presence of network failures, delays, or machine crashes.

a. Consensus Algorithms

In a distributed system, **consensus algorithms** ensure that all machines (or nodes) in the system agree on a single value or decision, even if some of the nodes are unreliable or fail. Consensus is critical for applications like databases, distributed ledgers (blockchains), and cloud computing.

Some popular consensus algorithms include:

- **Paxos**: A protocol for achieving consensus in a network of unreliable processors.
- **Raft**: A more understandable alternative to Paxos, used for managing replicated logs in distributed systems.
- **Practical Byzantine Fault Tolerance (PBFT)**: Used in scenarios where nodes might behave maliciously, such as blockchain systems.

b. Fault Tolerance

Fault tolerance is the ability of a system to continue functioning even when some of its components fail. In a distributed system, faults can occur due to network issues, hardware failures, or software bugs. Fault-tolerant systems are designed to handle these issues gracefully, ensuring the system remains operational despite partial failures.

For example:

- **Replication**: Data is stored on multiple nodes so that if one node fails, the data can still be accessed from another node.
- **Checkpointing**: The system periodically saves its state, so if a failure occurs, it can recover from the last saved state.
- **Heartbeat**: Nodes regularly send heartbeat messages to indicate they are alive, so the system can detect failures quickly.

4. Applications: Big Data Processing, Cloud Computing

Parallel and distributed algorithms have found extensive use in various domains, particularly where data is vast and computations are expensive. Some key applications include:

a. Big Data Processing

- In big data processing, the volume, velocity, and variety of data require parallel and distributed systems for processing. Tools like **Apache Hadoop** and **Apache Spark** leverage parallel and distributed algorithms for efficient data processing at scale.

b. Cloud Computing

- In cloud computing, distributed systems are used to ensure scalability, high availability, and fault tolerance. Cloud platforms like **AWS**, **Google Cloud**, and **Azure** employ distributed algorithms for resource management, load balancing, and database replication.

c. Machine Learning

- Machine learning models, particularly deep learning models, benefit from parallel and distributed computing. Large datasets and high computational requirements are handled by distributing tasks across multiple GPUs or machines. Frameworks like **TensorFlow** and **PyTorch** allow training models in parallel across distributed systems.

Parallel and distributed algorithms are indispensable for tackling modern computational problems, particularly in areas like big data, cloud computing, and machine learning. By efficiently dividing tasks across multiple processors or machines, we can handle problems that were previously infeasible due to computational or memory limitations. The examples discussed in this chapter, such as **MapReduce**, **Merge Sort**, and **Paxos**, show the potential of these techniques to solve complex, large-scale problems effectively.

In the next chapter, we'll explore **Greedy Algorithms**, a different paradigm for solving optimization problems where a series of locally optimal choices lead to a globally optimal solution.

CHAPTER 15: APPROXIMATION AND HEURISTIC ALGORITHMS

In the world of algorithm design, there are some problems that are **inherently difficult** or **impractical** to solve exactly within a reasonable time frame. These problems often fall into the category of **NP-hard** or **NP-complete**, meaning that finding an optimal solution for large instances is computationally infeasible. Instead of solving these problems exactly, we turn to **approximation algorithms** and **heuristics**, which offer practical, near-optimal solutions in a fraction of the time.

In this chapter, we'll explore approximation and heuristic algorithms in detail, focusing on real-world problems like the **Traveling Salesman Problem (TSP)** and **Vertex Cover**. We will also dive into popular heuristic techniques, such as **simulated annealing** and **genetic algorithms**, and examine their applications in areas like logistics, artificial intelligence, and game theory.

1. When Exact Solutions Are Impractical

Many real-world optimization problems cannot be solved exactly in a reasonable amount of time as they grow larger. These problems belong to **NP-hard** or **NP-complete** classes, which imply that there is no known algorithm that can find an optimal solution efficiently (in polynomial time) for large inputs.

- **NP-hard problems**: Problems for which no polynomial-time solution is known, and all problems in NP can be reduced to them.
- **NP-complete problems**: A subset of NP-hard problems that are both in NP and as hard as any problem in NP.

For instance, in problems like the **Traveling Salesman Problem (TSP)**, the goal is to find the shortest route that visits a set of cities and returns to the starting city. As the number of cities increases, the number of possible routes grows exponentially, making the problem infeasible to solve exactly for large inputs.

Similarly, **Vertex Cover** is another classic problem in which we need to select the smallest subset of vertices in a graph such that each edge is incident to at least one of the selected vertices. Again, finding the optimal solution for large graphs is impractical.

Instead of finding exact solutions, we can employ **approximation algorithms** and **heuristics** that provide good solutions in a reasonable amount of time.

2. Approximation Algorithms

Approximation algorithms are designed to find solutions that are close to the optimal, usually with guarantees about the performance of the solution relative to the optimal. These algorithms are typically used for **optimization problems** where finding the exact optimal solution is computationally expensive.

a. Traveling Salesman Problem (TSP)

The **Traveling Salesman Problem (TSP)** is a classical example of an NP-hard problem. The exact solution requires exploring all possible routes, which becomes infeasible as the number of cities increases.

- **Exact Solution**: If we want to find the optimal solution, we would have to check every possible combination of cities, leading to a factorial time complexity ($O(n!)$).

- **Approximation Solution**: In cases where an exact solution is impractical, we can use approximation algorithms to find a route that is near-optimal in polynomial time.

One well-known approximation algorithm for the TSP is the **Christofides algorithm**, which guarantees a solution within 1.5 times the optimal solution. The basic idea is to:

1. Find a minimum spanning tree (MST) of the cities.
2. Find a minimum-weight perfect matching for the odd-degree vertices in the MST.
3. Combine the MST and matching to form a Eulerian circuit and then convert it to a Hamiltonian circuit.

b. Vertex Cover

The **Vertex Cover** problem asks for the smallest set of vertices that cover all edges in a graph. It is also NP-complete, meaning finding the exact solution can be computationally expensive.

- **Exact Solution**: Brute-force methods would explore all combinations of vertices to check which set covers all edges, which would take exponential time.
- **Approximation Solution**: A common approximation algorithm for this problem is the **2-approximation algorithm**, which guarantees that the size of the vertex cover will be at most twice the size of the optimal solution.

The 2-approximation algorithm works as follows:

1. Start with an arbitrary edge in the graph.
2. Add both vertices of the edge to the vertex cover.
3. Remove all edges covered by these two vertices.
4. Repeat the process until no edges remain.

This algorithm is efficient, running in linear time with respect to the number of edges, and guarantees a solution within a factor of 2 of the optimal.

3. Heuristics: Finding Good Solutions Quickly

Heuristic algorithms are strategies used to find good-enough solutions to complex problems, especially when optimal solutions are difficult or impossible to compute. Unlike approximation algorithms, heuristics do not guarantee any specific performance bound but are often very efficient and provide good solutions in practice.

a. Simulated Annealing

Simulated Annealing is a heuristic inspired by the process of **annealing** in metallurgy, where a material is heated and then slowly cooled to reach a stable, low-energy state. In the context of algorithms, simulated annealing is used to find an approximation of the global optimum by exploring the solution space and probabilistically accepting worse solutions in the short term to avoid getting stuck in local optima.

The algorithm works by:

1. Randomly selecting an initial solution.
2. Iteratively making small changes to the solution.
3. Accepting the new solution if it improves the objective function or if a probability condition (based on the current temperature) is met, even if it worsens the objective.
4. Gradually reducing the "temperature" (probability of accepting worse solutions) until convergence.

Example: Traveling Salesman Problem

In the TSP, we can apply simulated annealing to explore possible routes, with the probability of accepting a worse route decreasing over time as the algorithm "cools" down.

python

```python
import random
import math

def simulated_annealing(problem, initial_solution, temperature, cooling_rate):
    current_solution = initial_solution
    current_cost = problem.cost(current_solution)

    while temperature > 1:
```

```
next_solution = problem.neighbor(current_solution)
next_cost = problem.cost(next_solution)


# If the new solution is better, accept it
if next_cost < current_cost:
    current_solution = next_solution
    current_cost = next_cost
else:
    # Accept worse solutions with a certain probability
    probability  =  math.exp((current_cost  -  next_cost)  /
temperature)
    if random.random() < probability:
        current_solution = next_solution
        current_cost = next_cost


# Cool down
temperature *= cooling_rate


return current_solution
```

b. Genetic Algorithms

Genetic Algorithms (GAs) are inspired by the process of natural selection. GAs work by evolving a population of potential solutions to a problem, selecting the best solutions, and using genetic operators such as **crossover** and **mutation** to generate new solutions.

Key steps in genetic algorithms include:

1. **Initialization**: Generate an initial population of potential solutions (often randomly).

2. **Selection**: Choose solutions that are fit (i.e., better solutions are more likely to be selected).

3. **Crossover**: Combine parts of two parent solutions to create offspring.

4. **Mutation**: Randomly modify a solution to maintain diversity in the population.

5. **Iteration**: Repeat the process for multiple generations until convergence.

Example: Solving the Knapsack Problem

In the knapsack problem, we aim to maximize the value of items placed in a knapsack while staying within a weight limit. A genetic algorithm could evolve a population of solutions (sets of items to include) and improve them over generations to find an optimal or near-optimal solution.

4. Real-World Applications of Heuristics and Approximation Algorithms

The power of approximation and heuristic algorithms lies in their ability to deliver practical solutions to real-world problems that are too complex for exact methods. Some notable applications include:

- **Logistics and Routing**: Problems like the **Traveling Salesman Problem** and **Vehicle Routing Problem** can be tackled using heuristic algorithms to optimize delivery routes and minimize travel time or costs.
- **AI and Game Theory**: Heuristics are widely used in AI, particularly in game theory for decision-making, such as in **chess** and **Go,** where the search space is too large to explore exhaustively. **Genetic algorithms** and **simulated annealing** are often used to optimize strategies in complex games.
- **Manufacturing and Supply Chain**: Approximation algorithms help in optimizing production schedules, inventory management, and supply chain routing.
- **Machine Learning**: Genetic algorithms and simulated annealing have been applied to feature selection, hyperparameter tuning, and model optimization in machine learning.

Approximation and heuristic algorithms are powerful tools for solving problems that are intractable with exact methods. By providing good-enough solutions efficiently, they enable practical applications in areas such as logistics, AI, game theory, and more. While they may not always guarantee the best possible solution, their speed and versatility make them invaluable in the modern computational landscape.

In the next chapter, we will explore **Greedy Algorithms**, another class of algorithms that can provide near-optimal solutions to many problems, often with simpler implementations and faster execution times.

CHAPTER 16: MACHINE LEARNING AND ALGORITHMS

Machine learning (ML) has emerged as one of the most transformative fields in computer science, driving innovations in fields like natural language processing, computer vision, and recommendation systems. At its core, ML is about creating models that can learn patterns from data and make predictions or decisions without being explicitly programmed. These models are built on a foundation of well-established **algorithms**.

In this chapter, we will explore how machine learning leverages algorithms, focusing on the differences between **supervised** and

unsupervised learning, and examining key algorithms like **decision trees**, **random forests**, and **clustering techniques**. Finally, we'll look at practical applications such as **recommendation systems** and **fraud detection**.

1. How Machine Learning Leverages Algorithms

Machine learning is heavily dependent on algorithms to process data, identify patterns, and generate predictions. These algorithms can be thought of as the mathematical backbone of ML, defining how the model learns and generalizes from data.

- **Data Preprocessing Algorithms**: These include methods for cleaning, normalizing, and transforming raw data into a format suitable for training machine learning models.
- **Optimization Algorithms**: Algorithms like gradient descent are used to minimize the error or loss of a model during training.
- **Learning Algorithms**: These include specific methods for building models from data, such as decision trees, support vector machines, and clustering algorithms.

At a high level, ML algorithms are used to:

1. Learn relationships between input features and target outcomes (supervised learning).

2. Discover hidden structures in unlabeled data (unsupervised learning).

3. Optimize complex decision-making processes (reinforcement learning, not covered here).

2. Supervised Learning: Decision Trees and Random Forests

In **supervised learning**, the goal is to learn a mapping from inputs (features) to outputs (labels) based on labeled training data. Two popular algorithms in supervised learning are **decision trees** and **random forests**.

a. Decision Trees

A **decision tree** is a flowchart-like structure where each internal node represents a feature (or attribute), each branch represents a decision rule, and each leaf node represents an outcome (label). Decision trees are used for both classification and regression tasks.

How It Works:

1. Start at the root node and split the dataset based on the feature that results in the greatest information gain or the least impurity (e.g., Gini index or entropy).

2. Recursively split the dataset at each child node until all data points in a node belong to the same class or a stopping criterion is met (e.g., maximum depth of the tree).

Advantages:

- Simple to understand and interpret.
- Handles both numerical and categorical data.
- Can model non-linear relationships.

Limitations:

- Prone to overfitting if the tree is too deep.
- Sensitive to small changes in data.

Example of a Decision Tree (Classification): A decision tree could classify whether a customer will buy a product based on features like age, income, and browsing behavior.

b. Random Forests

A **random forest** is an ensemble learning method that builds multiple decision trees and combines their predictions to improve accuracy and reduce overfitting. It leverages **bagging (bootstrap aggregating)** to create random subsets of the data and train individual trees on these subsets.

How It Works:

1. Generate multiple bootstrap samples (random subsets with replacement) from the training data.

2. Build a decision tree for each subset, where each split considers only a random subset of features.

3. Combine the predictions from all trees (e.g., majority voting for classification or averaging for regression).

Advantages:

- Reduces overfitting compared to individual decision trees.
- Handles large datasets with high dimensionality.
- Robust to noisy data and missing values.

Applications of Decision Trees and Random Forests:

- **Fraud Detection**: Identify fraudulent transactions by learning patterns of normal and anomalous behavior.
- **Medical Diagnosis**: Predict diseases based on patient symptoms and medical history.

3. Unsupervised Learning: Clustering Algorithms

In **unsupervised learning**, there are no labels or target outcomes. The goal is to find hidden structures or groupings within the data. A key family of algorithms in unsupervised learning is **clustering algorithms**, which group similar data points into clusters.

a. K-Means Clustering

K-means is one of the simplest and most popular clustering algorithms. It partitions data into kkk clusters, where each cluster is represented by its centroid (mean).

How It Works:

1. Initialize kkk centroids randomly.
2. Assign each data point to the nearest centroid.
3. Recalculate centroids as the mean of all data points in each cluster.
4. Repeat steps 2 and 3 until centroids stabilize or a maximum number of iterations is reached.

Applications:

- **Customer Segmentation**: Group customers based on purchasing behavior.
- **Image Compression**: Reduce the number of colors in an image by clustering pixels with similar colors.

b. Hierarchical Clustering

Hierarchical clustering builds a hierarchy of clusters by either:

- **Agglomerative (bottom-up)**: Start with each data point as its own cluster and merge the closest clusters iteratively.
- **Divisive (top-down)**: Start with one large cluster and recursively split it into smaller clusters.

The result is a **dendrogram**, a tree-like structure that visualizes the cluster hierarchy.

Applications:

- **Document Organization**: Group similar articles or documents.
- **Social Network Analysis**: Identify communities or groups of friends.

c. DBSCAN (Density-Based Spatial Clustering of Applications with Noise)

DBSCAN groups data points based on density, making it effective for identifying clusters of arbitrary shapes and handling noise.

How It Works:

1. Identify core points (points with a minimum number of neighbors within a radius).
2. Expand clusters from core points by including reachable points.
3. Label points that don't belong to any cluster as noise.

Applications:

- **Anomaly Detection**: Detect outliers in datasets (e.g., fraudulent transactions).

- **Geospatial Analysis**: Identify dense areas in geographic data.

4. Applications of Machine Learning Algorithms

Machine learning algorithms power a wide range of real-world applications, revolutionizing industries such as e-commerce, finance, healthcare, and more. Below are some key examples:

a. Recommendation Systems

- Algorithms like decision trees, clustering, and collaborative filtering are used to recommend products, movies, or services to users.
- **Example**: Amazon and Netflix suggest products or movies based on user preferences and behavior.

b. Fraud Detection

- Supervised learning algorithms like random forests are used to identify patterns of fraudulent activity in financial transactions.
- **Example**: Banks use ML to detect credit card fraud by recognizing unusual spending patterns.

c. Customer Segmentation

- Clustering algorithms like K-means are used to group customers based on behavior, demographics, or purchasing patterns.
- **Example**: Retailers use segmentation to design targeted marketing campaigns.

d. Medical Diagnosis

- Decision trees and random forests are used to predict diseases based on symptoms and test results.
- **Example**: ML models help radiologists identify tumors in medical images.

e. Image and Speech Recognition

- Neural networks (covered in later chapters) are heavily used for recognizing faces, objects, and speech.
- **Example**: Virtual assistants like Siri and Alexa rely on ML algorithms for voice recognition.

5. Performance Considerations

While ML algorithms are powerful, their performance depends on:

- **Quality of Data**: Poor-quality or biased data can lead to inaccurate predictions.

- **Hyperparameter Tuning**: Algorithms like random forests and clustering require tuning parameters (e.g., number of trees, number of clusters) for optimal performance.
- **Computational Complexity**: Algorithms like random forests can be computationally expensive, especially for large datasets.

Machine learning leverages algorithms like decision trees, random forests, and clustering techniques to solve a wide variety of problems, from classification and regression to grouping and anomaly detection. These algorithms form the backbone of many applications in e-commerce, healthcare, and beyond. By understanding their principles, strengths, and limitations, you can apply them effectively to real-world challenges.

In the next chapter, we'll explore **Dynamic Programming**, an essential technique for solving problems with overlapping subproblems and optimal substructure, which complements the algorithms discussed in this chapter.

CHAPTER 17: ALGORITHMS IN PRACTICE: REAL-WORLD APPLICATIONS

Algorithms are not just abstract concepts confined to theoretical computer science—they are the engines driving some of the most impactful and innovative systems in the modern world. From optimizing e-commerce platforms to revolutionizing healthcare and enabling breakthroughs in fintech, algorithms are integral to solving real-world problems at scale. In this chapter, we'll explore practical case studies, strategies for building scalable systems with efficient algorithms, and the future of algorithms, including the roles of AI and quantum computing.

1. Case Studies: Algorithms in E-Commerce, Healthcare, and Fintech

a. Algorithms in E-Commerce

E-commerce platforms like Amazon, Alibaba, and Shopify rely heavily on algorithms to improve customer experiences and optimize operations. Key algorithmic applications include:

- **Recommendation Systems**: Algorithms like collaborative filtering and matrix factorization suggest products to users based on their preferences and behavior.
  - **Example**: Amazon's "Customers Who Bought This Also Bought" feature uses collaborative filtering to predict user interests.
- **Dynamic Pricing**: Algorithms adjust prices in real time based on demand, competition, and inventory.
  - **Example**: Airlines and ride-sharing apps like Uber use dynamic pricing algorithms to maximize revenue while staying competitive.
- **Supply Chain Optimization**: Algorithms optimize inventory management, logistics, and delivery routes.
  - **Example**: Warehouse robots powered by pathfinding algorithms like A* help Amazon streamline order fulfillment.

b. Algorithms in Healthcare

In healthcare, algorithms are transforming patient care, diagnostics, and operational efficiency:

- **Medical Imaging**: Algorithms such as convolutional neural networks (CNNs) analyze X-rays, MRIs, and CT scans to detect abnormalities like tumors or fractures.
  - ○ **Example**: Deep learning algorithms are used to detect cancer in mammograms with accuracy comparable to human radiologists.
- **Predictive Analytics**: Machine learning algorithms predict patient outcomes, helping doctors make informed decisions.
  - ○ **Example**: Hospitals use predictive models to identify patients at risk of readmission, enabling preemptive interventions.
- **Drug Discovery**: Algorithms accelerate drug discovery by analyzing molecular data and simulating interactions.
  - ○ **Example**: AI-driven algorithms like AlphaFold predict protein structures, aiding in the development of new drugs.

c. Algorithms in Fintech

The financial industry leverages algorithms to drive efficiency, enhance security, and make informed decisions:

- **Fraud Detection**: Algorithms analyze transaction patterns to identify anomalies indicative of fraud.

o **Example**: Credit card companies use machine learning models like random forests to flag unusual transactions.

- **Algorithmic Trading**: High-frequency trading systems execute trades in milliseconds using algorithms to capitalize on market trends.

    o **Example**: Quantitative trading firms use algorithms like moving averages and mean reversion strategies to maximize returns.

- **Credit Scoring**: Algorithms assess creditworthiness by analyzing financial data and behaviors.

    o **Example**: Fintech companies like Affirm and Klarna use AI-driven models to approve loans in real time.

2. Building Scalable Systems with Efficient Algorithms

Scalability is critical when deploying algorithms in real-world systems. As the scale of data and users grows, poorly designed algorithms can lead to bottlenecks and inefficiencies. Here are key principles for building scalable systems:

a. Algorithmic Efficiency

- Choose algorithms with optimal time and space complexity for the problem at hand.

- o **Example**: Use hash tables ($O(1)O(1)O(1)$) for quick lookups instead of binary search ($O(\log n)O(\log n)O(\log n)$) when possible.
- Prioritize algorithms that work well with distributed computing frameworks like **MapReduce** or **Apache Spark**.
  - o **Example**: For big data analytics, parallel algorithms for sorting or aggregating data improve performance.

b. Data Structures

- Use appropriate data structures to complement algorithms. For example:
  - o **Graphs** for modeling networks (e.g., social connections, transportation).
  - o **Heaps** for priority-based tasks like scheduling.
  - o **Tries** for efficient string searches.

c. Distributed Systems

- Algorithms must be designed to handle distributed environments, ensuring fault tolerance and consistency.
  - o **Example**: Consensus algorithms like **Paxos** or **Raft** ensure reliability in distributed databases.

d. Optimization Techniques

- Implement caching and memoization to reduce redundant computations.

  o **Example**: Use dynamic programming to optimize recursive algorithms in applications like route planning.

- Use approximate algorithms when exact solutions are computationally infeasible.

  o **Example**: In recommendation systems, collaborative filtering can be approximated using matrix factorization.

3. The Future of Algorithms: AI and Quantum Computing

The landscape of algorithms is rapidly evolving, with advancements in AI and quantum computing opening new frontiers.

a. Artificial Intelligence

- **AI Algorithms**: Algorithms like neural networks, reinforcement learning, and generative adversarial networks (GANs) are driving breakthroughs in areas like natural language processing (e.g., ChatGPT), computer vision, and autonomous systems.

  o **Example**: GPT models use transformer architectures to understand and generate human-like text.

- **AI-Driven Optimization**: AI algorithms are being used to improve classical algorithms by learning from patterns in data.

    o **Example**: Metaheuristic algorithms powered by AI are solving complex optimization problems in logistics and manufacturing.

b. Quantum Computing

Quantum computing promises to revolutionize algorithms by leveraging quantum phenomena such as superposition and entanglement. Key areas of impact include:

- **Quantum Search Algorithms**: Grover's algorithm can search unsorted databases in $O(N)O(\sqrt{N})O(N)$, compared to $O(N)O(N)O(N)$ for classical search.

- **Quantum Cryptography**: Algorithms like Shor's algorithm can factorize large numbers exponentially faster, potentially breaking classical encryption schemes like RSA.

- **Optimization**: Quantum algorithms can solve optimization problems, such as the Traveling Salesman Problem, more efficiently using quantum annealing.

4. Practical Advice for Choosing and Implementing Algorithms

When deploying algorithms in real-world systems, the following guidelines can help ensure success:

a. Understand the Problem

- Clearly define the problem and constraints. This ensures that you choose the most appropriate algorithm.
  - **Example**: For a shortest-path problem, use Dijkstra's algorithm for graphs with non-negative weights and Bellman-Ford for graphs with negative weights.

b. Balance Performance and Complexity

- Choose algorithms that strike a balance between efficiency and implementation complexity.
  - **Example**: QuickSort is easier to implement than MergeSort but has worse performance in the worst case.

c. Profile and Optimize

- Use profiling tools to identify bottlenecks and optimize algorithmic performance.
  - **Example**: Python's cProfile can help pinpoint slow parts of your code.

d. Test at Scale

- Test algorithms with large datasets to ensure scalability.

- o **Example**: A hashing-based solution might work well for small datasets but could degrade with hash collisions as the dataset grows.

e. Consider Approximation

- If exact solutions are impractical, consider approximation or heuristic algorithms.
  - o **Example**: Use greedy algorithms for the knapsack problem when exact solutions are infeasible.

Algorithms are the driving force behind modern technology, enabling scalable, efficient, and intelligent systems in industries ranging from e-commerce to healthcare and fintech. By understanding real-world applications, choosing efficient algorithms, and anticipating future advancements like AI and quantum computing, you can harness the full potential of algorithms to solve complex problems.

In the next chapter, we'll conclude this exploration of algorithms by summarizing key takeaways and offering guidance on how to continue building expertise in algorithm design and application.

CHAPTER 18: CONCLUSION: HARNESSING THE POWER OF ALGORITHMS

As we conclude this exploration of algorithms, it's clear that they are much more than theoretical constructs—they are the engines that power the digital age, enabling us to solve problems efficiently, scale systems globally, and innovate in ways previously unimaginable. From classical approaches like divide-and-conquer and dynamic programming to modern advancements in machine learning and quantum computing, algorithms form the backbone of computational problem-solving.

This chapter synthesizes the key takeaways from the book, provides guidance for implementing algorithms in real-world scenarios, and highlights the future directions of algorithmic research and application.

1. Key Takeaways

Through the preceding chapters, we've examined a wide variety of algorithmic paradigms, tools, and applications. Here are the core insights:

a. Algorithmic Foundations

- Understanding **data structures** (e.g., arrays, trees, graphs) is critical for designing efficient algorithms.
- Fundamental paradigms like **greedy algorithms**, **dynamic programming**, and **divide-and-conquer** offer structured approaches to solving diverse problems.

b. Specialized Techniques

- **Backtracking** and **heuristic algorithms** help solve combinatorial problems like the Traveling Salesman Problem when exact solutions are infeasible.
- **Approximation algorithms** provide near-optimal solutions for NP-hard problems within guaranteed bounds.

c. Advanced Applications

- Algorithms are integral to **machine learning**, where supervised and unsupervised techniques like decision trees, clustering, and neural networks unlock insights from data.
- **Parallel and distributed algorithms** enable scalable systems, powering applications in big data, cloud computing, and real-time systems.

d. Scalability and Efficiency

- The efficiency of an algorithm depends not only on its time and space complexity but also on how it integrates with the system architecture, such as distributed or cloud-based environments.
- **Optimization techniques** like caching, memoization, and preprocessing can significantly enhance performance.

2. Practical Guidance for Algorithm Implementation

a. Problem Understanding

- Clearly define the problem, inputs, outputs, and constraints before selecting an algorithmic approach.
- Identify whether the problem requires an exact solution or if an approximation or heuristic will suffice.

b. Algorithm Selection

- Match the algorithm to the problem type:
  - **Sorting and searching**: Use QuickSort, MergeSort, or Binary Search.
  - **Graph problems**: Apply Dijkstra's for shortest paths or Prim's for minimum spanning trees.
  - **Optimization**: Use dynamic programming for overlapping subproblems or greedy algorithms for locally optimal choices.

c. Implementation

- Use libraries and frameworks when appropriate to save development time:
  - Python's NumPy for matrix operations.
  - NetworkX for graph algorithms.
  - Machine learning libraries like scikit-learn for decision trees and clustering.

d. Testing and Profiling

- Test algorithms with small datasets for correctness, then scale up to real-world sizes to ensure performance.
- Use profiling tools like Python's cProfile or Java's VisualVM to identify bottlenecks and optimize performance.

3. The Future of Algorithms

The field of algorithms is continually evolving, driven by advancements in hardware, software, and the complexity of real-world problems. Here are some key trends shaping the future:

a. AI-Driven Algorithms

- Algorithms are increasingly integrated with AI to adapt and learn from data. Techniques like **reinforcement learning** and **meta-learning** are paving the way for algorithms that optimize themselves based on context.

b. Quantum Computing

- As quantum hardware matures, algorithms designed for quantum systems, such as **Shor's algorithm** for factoring and **Grover's algorithm** for search, promise exponential speedups for specific problem classes.

c. Ethical and Transparent Algorithms

- With algorithms influencing decisions in critical areas like hiring, healthcare, and criminal justice, there is a growing demand for fairness, transparency, and accountability in algorithm design.

d. Algorithmic Creativity

- Algorithms are being used for creative purposes, such as generating art, music, and even writing. Tools like **generative adversarial networks (GANs)** and **transformers** are at the forefront of this revolution.

4. Building Expertise in Algorithms

For anyone looking to deepen their understanding and application of algorithms, the following steps are essential:

a. Learn by Doing

- Practice solving problems on competitive programming platforms like **LeetCode**, **HackerRank**, or **Codeforces**.
- Implement algorithms from scratch to gain a deeper understanding of their mechanics.

b. Study Real-World Systems

- Analyze how companies like Google, Amazon, and Netflix implement algorithms in search, recommendations, and optimization.

c. Stay Updated

- Follow research in fields like machine learning, quantum computing, and computational biology to see how algorithms are evolving.

d. Collaborate

- Participate in hackathons, coding competitions, and open-source projects to gain practical experience and learn from others.

5. Conclusion

Algorithms are more than just tools for problem-solving—they are the foundation of innovation in technology, science, and industry. By mastering the principles, exploring advanced techniques, and applying them to real-world problems, you can unlock the potential of algorithms to drive progress and efficiency in any domain.

As we stand on the cusp of new advancements in AI, quantum computing, and distributed systems, the role of algorithms will only grow more significant. Whether you're an aspiring developer, a researcher, or a seasoned professional, the journey into the world of algorithms offers endless opportunities to create, optimize, and innovate.

This concludes the exploration of algorithms. The next step is to take these insights and apply them to your own challenges, whether through research, development, or real-world problem-solving. The power of algorithms is in your hands—use it wisely and creatively.

CHAPTER 19: ALGORITHMS IN PRACTICE: REAL-WORLD APPLICATIONS

In this chapter, we will explore how the algorithms we've studied are applied in the real world. While understanding algorithmic theory is important, knowing how to effectively use algorithms to solve practical problems is equally crucial. Whether in e-commerce, healthcare, finance, or artificial intelligence, algorithms power many of the systems and tools that we interact with every day.

By analyzing case studies and practical applications, we'll see how different algorithms solve complex problems and contribute to the efficiency, scalability, and innovation of modern systems.

1. Case Studies of Algorithms in Practice

a. E-Commerce and Recommendation Systems

One of the most prominent applications of algorithms in modern technology is in e-commerce. Websites like Amazon and Netflix use complex recommendation systems to suggest products or content to users, based on their browsing history, purchase behavior, and preferences. These systems rely heavily on **collaborative filtering** and **content-based filtering** algorithms.

- **Collaborative filtering**: This algorithm finds similarities between users based on shared preferences and suggests items that similar users have liked. For example, if you and another user bought the same items, the algorithm may recommend additional products that the other user purchased but you haven't yet.
- **Content-based filtering**: In contrast, this algorithm suggests products based on their attributes. For instance, if you frequently purchase books in the mystery genre, the system will recommend other mystery novels.

Amazon also uses **search algorithms** to help customers find products quickly, utilizing **text search**, **ranking algorithms**, and **optimization techniques** for relevancy and speed.

b. Healthcare and Predictive Analytics

In healthcare, algorithms are increasingly used for **predictive analytics**, which involves predicting patient outcomes, disease progression, and more. These systems rely on machine learning algorithms to analyze vast amounts of patient data, such as medical histories, genetic data, and test results, to predict future health risks.

- **Clinical Decision Support Systems (CDSS)**: These systems help doctors make decisions about treatment by analyzing a patient's medical history and comparing it to a large database of similar cases. Machine learning algorithms, such as **logistic regression**, **support vector machines (SVMs)**, and **random forests**, are commonly used for such predictive tasks.

- **Medical image analysis**: Algorithms like **Convolutional Neural Networks (CNNs)** are used to analyze medical images (e.g., MRIs, X-rays) for signs of diseases like cancer or heart conditions.

For example, algorithms can identify early signs of lung cancer in CT scans, far earlier than a radiologist might detect it. This predictive power can save lives by allowing for earlier treatment and interventions.

c. Finance and Fraud Detection

Financial institutions use algorithms for a variety of tasks, from automating trades to analyzing risks and detecting fraud. In fraud detection, machine learning algorithms analyze patterns in transaction data and flag any suspicious activity.

- **Fraud detection algorithms**: Algorithms track financial transactions in real-time, identifying anomalies based on known patterns of fraudulent activity. For example, if a credit card is used in two different countries within an hour, the algorithm may flag this as suspicious. Commonly used algorithms include **decision trees**, **logistic regression**, and **anomaly detection models**.

- **Algorithmic trading**: In stock markets, trading strategies are increasingly automated through the use of **high-frequency trading algorithms**. These algorithms can analyze market trends and execute trades at speeds much faster than humans, capitalizing on small fluctuations in stock prices. Algorithms like **statistical arbitrage** and **market-making algorithms** are used for this purpose.

- **Risk analysis**: In risk management, algorithms are used to model and predict financial risks. For example, the **Value at Risk (VaR)** model uses historical data and statistical techniques to calculate the potential loss in the value of a portfolio over a given time period with a certain confidence level.

d. Autonomous Vehicles

In autonomous vehicles, algorithms play a central role in enabling self-driving cars to navigate complex environments. These algorithms process data from sensors (such as cameras, LIDAR, and radar) and make real-time decisions about speed, direction, and obstacles.

- **Computer vision algorithms**: Algorithms like **Object Detection** (e.g., YOLO - You Only Look Once) and **Semantic Segmentation** are used to interpret visual data from cameras, helping the vehicle understand its surroundings.

- **Path planning algorithms**: Algorithms like *A search** and **Dijkstra's algorithm** are used to find the optimal path for the car to take, avoiding obstacles while minimizing travel time.

- **Reinforcement learning**: Some advanced self-driving systems use reinforcement learning to continuously improve their decision-making by learning from each interaction with the environment.

Tesla, Waymo, and other companies at the forefront of autonomous driving are using a combination of these algorithms to make self-driving cars safer and more efficient.

e. Social Media and Content Moderation

Social media platforms like Facebook, Twitter, and Instagram use algorithms to decide which posts users see and how content is filtered. Algorithms analyze user behavior and interactions to curate personalized feeds, prioritize posts, and even flag inappropriate content.

- **Personalized feed algorithms**: These systems use collaborative filtering, content-based filtering, and ranking algorithms to present content that aligns with users' interests and previous interactions.
- **Content moderation algorithms**: Social media platforms use **Natural Language Processing (NLP)** and **image recognition algorithms** to detect harmful content, including hate speech, fake news, or graphic violence. These systems flag potentially inappropriate content, which is then reviewed by human moderators.

While these algorithms are effective at processing large amounts of data, they also raise ethical concerns, particularly around bias and censorship.

2. Building Scalable Systems with Efficient Algorithms

In real-world applications, scalability and efficiency are critical. As data grows and user numbers increase, algorithms must be able to handle larger volumes of data without slowing down or running into computational bottlenecks.

a. Distributed Algorithms

Many modern systems require the use of distributed algorithms to process data across multiple machines. This is especially true in systems like cloud computing, databases, and big data processing platforms. Examples include:

- **MapReduce**: A programming model for processing large data sets in parallel across a distributed cluster. It divides the data into smaller chunks, processes them in parallel, and then reduces the results.
- **Consensus algorithms**: These algorithms ensure that distributed systems agree on a single source of truth, such as in blockchain systems. Algorithms like **Paxos** and **Raft** are used to maintain consistency in distributed systems.

b. Load Balancing and Caching

In large-scale systems, **load balancing** algorithms distribute incoming requests across multiple servers to ensure that no single server is overwhelmed. This improves system availability and reliability.

- **Round-robin** and **least connection** are examples of load-balancing algorithms.
- **Caching algorithms** like **Least Recently Used (LRU)** are used to store frequently accessed data in memory, speeding up access times for commonly requested data.

3. The Future of Algorithms

Algorithms are constantly evolving, driven by innovations in technology and the increasing complexity of the problems they aim to solve. Looking ahead, we can expect several key developments in algorithmic design:

- **Quantum Algorithms**: As quantum computing advances, new algorithms designed to take advantage of quantum properties will emerge. Quantum algorithms like **Shor's algorithm** and **Grover's algorithm** promise to revolutionize fields like cryptography and search.
- **AI-Driven Algorithms**: The intersection of algorithms and machine learning will continue to grow. Algorithms that can learn and adapt to new data will be increasingly used in domains like healthcare, robotics, and personalized marketing.
- **Ethical Algorithms**: As algorithms become more pervasive, the focus on fairness, transparency, and accountability will increase. Ensuring that algorithms do

not perpetuate biases and that their decision-making processes are understandable will be paramount.

Algorithms are the foundation of modern technology, enabling everything from personalized recommendations to self-driving cars. By studying real-world applications, we've seen how algorithms are not just abstract concepts but practical tools that solve problems, improve efficiency, and drive innovation.

As we continue to advance in the fields of machine learning, artificial intelligence, and quantum computing, algorithms will only become more powerful and central to our daily lives. Whether you're a developer, data scientist, or just an enthusiast, mastering algorithms is the key to understanding and shaping the future of technology.

CHAPTER 20: PARALLEL AND DISTRIBUTED ALGORITHMS

In the world of modern computing, the need for efficiency, speed, and scalability has led to the development of **parallel and distributed algorithms**. These algorithms enable systems to process data and execute tasks simultaneously, making them crucial for solving large-scale, complex problems across multiple machines or processors. From big data processing to cloud computing, parallel and distributed algorithms are fundamental to the performance of a wide range of systems.

In this chapter, we will explore the concepts behind parallel and distributed algorithms, how they differ, and the challenges associated with implementing them. We will also look at some key paradigms and techniques, such as **MapReduce, divide-and-conquer, consensus algorithms**, and **fault tolerance**, and illustrate them with practical examples and real-world applications.

1. The Need for Parallel and Distributed Systems

As computational problems grow in size and complexity, single-machine systems often reach their limits in terms of processing power and memory capacity. To handle large datasets, complex computations, or high-throughput tasks, we need to leverage the combined power of multiple processing units (processors, cores, or machines). This is where **parallel computing** and **distributed computing** come into play.

- **Parallel computing** involves breaking a problem into smaller subproblems and solving them simultaneously using multiple processors or cores within a single machine.
- **Distributed computing**, on the other hand, involves distributing different parts of a computation across multiple

machines (or nodes), each working on its part of the task, and then combining the results.

Both approaches aim to speed up computation, improve scalability, and ensure that systems can handle large-scale tasks without bottlenecks. These systems are crucial for applications such as:

- **Big data processing** (e.g., Hadoop, Spark)
- **Scientific simulations** (e.g., climate modeling, molecular dynamics)
- **Real-time data analytics** (e.g., stock market analysis, IoT systems)
- **Machine learning** and **deep learning** training on large datasets

2. Parallel Algorithms

Parallel algorithms break a problem into smaller subproblems, each of which can be executed concurrently. The key to successful parallelization is identifying the parts of a problem that can be performed in parallel without dependencies.

a. Divide and Conquer in Parallel

One of the most common strategies for parallel computing is the **divide-and-conquer** paradigm. This approach involves dividing a problem into smaller subproblems, solving each subproblem in parallel, and then combining the results.

- **Merge Sort** and **Quick Sort** are classic examples of divide-and-conquer algorithms. By splitting the data into smaller chunks, sorting each chunk in parallel, and then merging the sorted chunks, these algorithms can achieve significant speedup in a parallel environment.
- **Matrix Multiplication**: In computational mathematics, matrix multiplication is a commonly parallelized task. The algorithm splits the multiplication into sub-matrices, with each sub-matrix computed by a separate processor, and the results combined afterward.

b. MapReduce

One of the most well-known frameworks for parallel processing is **MapReduce**. Originally popularized by Google, MapReduce is a programming model that allows for processing large datasets across distributed clusters of computers.

The MapReduce model has two main phases:

- **Map phase**: The input data is divided into smaller chunks, and a map function is applied to each chunk. Each chunk is processed independently and can be executed in parallel across different machines or processors.

- **Reduce phase**: After the map phase, the output from each map task is grouped by a key. The reduce function then aggregates the results, often producing a summary or a final output.

MapReduce is widely used for applications such as **log file analysis**, **search indexing**, **data mining**, and **machine learning** model training.

c. Parallel Sorting Algorithms

Sorting is one of the most commonly parallelized operations, especially when working with large datasets. **Parallel merge sort** and **parallel quicksort** are two examples of sorting algorithms that break the sorting task into multiple independent subproblems that can be solved in parallel.

For example, in parallel merge sort, the data is recursively divided into halves, and each half is sorted in parallel. Once the subarrays are sorted, they are merged in parallel, reducing the time complexity from $O(n \log n)$ in the sequential version to $O(\log n)$ for the parallel version, depending on the number of processors available.

3. Distributed Algorithms

While parallel algorithms focus on utilizing multiple processors or cores within a single machine, **distributed algorithms** are designed to solve problems across multiple machines in a network.

These algorithms must account for the challenges of communication, fault tolerance, and coordination between distributed systems.

a. Consensus Algorithms

A major challenge in distributed computing is achieving consensus—ensuring that all nodes in a distributed system agree on a single value or decision. Consensus algorithms are used in scenarios such as distributed databases, blockchain, and coordination systems.

- **Paxos** and **Raft** are two well-known consensus algorithms. They are designed to ensure that, even if some nodes fail or messages are lost, the distributed system can still reach an agreement on the next action or decision.
  - **Paxos** is known for its fault tolerance and ensuring consistency in distributed systems, but it is often criticized for being complex to implement.
  - **Raft** is a more recent algorithm designed to be easier to understand and implement while still ensuring strong consistency and fault tolerance.

These algorithms are critical for maintaining the integrity and reliability of distributed systems, such as distributed databases (e.g., Cassandra, etcd) or blockchain networks (e.g., Bitcoin).

b. Fault Tolerance

Fault tolerance in distributed algorithms ensures that the system can continue functioning even in the presence of node failures, network partitions, or other issues. Distributed algorithms must be designed with redundancy, replication, and error detection in mind.

- **Replicated databases** often use algorithms to replicate data across multiple nodes, so that if one node fails, others can take over.
- **MapReduce** and **Hadoop** are designed with fault tolerance by duplicating tasks and storing intermediate results across multiple machines to prevent data loss.

c. Distributed Coordination

In distributed systems, coordination between different nodes is essential for ensuring consistency and correctness. Algorithms like **Two-Phase Commit (2PC)** and **Three-Phase Commit (3PC)** are used in distributed databases to ensure that transactions are completed in a consistent and atomic manner.

These coordination protocols help maintain consistency and prevent data corruption in systems where transactions involve multiple nodes.

4. Challenges in Parallel and Distributed Algorithms

While parallel and distributed algorithms offer significant performance improvements, they come with a set of challenges:

a. Synchronization

In parallel algorithms, especially when multiple threads or processes are involved, synchronization becomes a critical issue. Ensuring that different parts of a computation do not conflict with each other (e.g., by updating the same data concurrently) is a fundamental concern. Common techniques to handle synchronization include **locks**, **mutexes**, and **semaphores**.

b. Load Balancing

In distributed systems, **load balancing** ensures that tasks are evenly distributed across all nodes or processors, avoiding situations where some nodes are overloaded while others are underutilized. Techniques like **round-robin** and **least-loaded** are commonly used to balance workloads in distributed systems.

c. Scalability

Scalability refers to a system's ability to handle increasing loads by adding more resources (processors, machines, etc.) without a significant drop in performance. Algorithms must be designed with scalability in mind, especially when working with distributed or cloud-based systems.

5. *Real-World Applications of Parallel and Distributed Algorithms*

a. Big Data Processing

In big data applications, parallel and distributed algorithms are used to process vast amounts of data. Frameworks like **Hadoop** and **Apache Spark** use distributed algorithms to perform operations on data spread across a cluster of machines. These systems are used in industries like healthcare (e.g., analyzing patient records), retail (e.g., analyzing customer behavior), and finance (e.g., detecting fraudulent transactions).

b. Cloud Computing

Cloud computing platforms, such as **Amazon Web Services (AWS)** and **Microsoft Azure**, rely on parallel and distributed algorithms to provide elastic computing resources to users. By distributing computing tasks across multiple virtual machines, these systems can dynamically scale to meet demand, ensuring high availability and fault tolerance.

c. Machine Learning

Machine learning algorithms are often parallelized to handle large datasets more efficiently. **Distributed training** of models (such as deep learning models) is made possible by parallel and distributed computing. For instance, **TensorFlow** and **PyTorch** support distributed training, allowing large models to be trained across multiple GPUs or machines.

Parallel and distributed algorithms are essential for solving large-scale problems efficiently in today's data-driven world. By leveraging multiple processors or machines, these algorithms enable faster computations, better scalability, and greater fault tolerance. Whether you're working with big data, cloud systems, or machine learning, understanding the fundamentals of parallel and distributed computing will help you design more efficient and robust systems.

As computational problems become increasingly complex and the demand for real-time processing grows, parallel and distributed algorithms will continue to play a critical role in shaping the future of technology.

CHAPTER 21: INTRODUCTION TO BLOCKCHAIN AND CRYPTOCURRENCIES

The rise of blockchain technology and cryptocurrencies has revolutionized multiple sectors, from finance and supply chains to digital identity and beyond. At its core, blockchain is a decentralized, secure, and transparent way of storing and transferring data, while cryptocurrencies are digital assets that use blockchain for their transactions. This chapter will provide an in-depth exploration of both technologies, explain how they work, and discuss the algorithms that power them. By the end of this chapter, you'll have a solid understanding of how blockchain and cryptocurrencies function, their real-world applications, and how to work with cryptocurrency data using Python.

1. Overview of Blockchain Technology

Blockchain is a distributed ledger technology that securely records transactions across a network of computers. The key features that make blockchain particularly unique are its **decentralization**, **immutability**, and **transparency**.

- **Decentralization**: Unlike traditional databases that are controlled by a single authority (such as a bank or government), blockchain relies on a network of computers (called nodes) that all hold copies of the ledger. This reduces the risk of fraud, censorship, and failure because there is no single point of control.

- **Immutability**: Once data is recorded in a blockchain, it cannot be altered or deleted. Each block of data is cryptographically linked to the previous block, creating a chain of blocks. This ensures that the data is tamper-resistant, as any attempt to change data would require altering all subsequent blocks, which is computationally infeasible.

- **Transparency**: Blockchain offers transparency because the ledger is open and accessible to all participants in the network, ensuring that transactions can be verified by anyone. Public blockchains like Bitcoin and Ethereum allow anyone to view transaction history, while private blockchains restrict access to certain participants.

How Blockchain Works:

Blockchain operates through the following steps:

1. **Transaction initiation**: A user initiates a transaction by sending data (e.g., transferring cryptocurrency) to the network.

2. **Transaction verification**: The transaction is broadcast to the network, where it is verified by nodes using a consensus algorithm (e.g., Proof of Work or Proof of Stake).

3. **Block creation**: Once verified, the transaction is grouped with other transactions into a block.

4. **Block addition to the chain**: The block is added to the existing blockchain, becoming part of the permanent ledger.

5. **Consensus**: The network reaches consensus, confirming that the transaction is valid and adding it to the blockchain.

2. Cryptocurrencies: Digital Assets on the Blockchain

Cryptocurrencies are digital or virtual currencies that use cryptographic techniques to secure transactions and control the creation of new units. Cryptocurrencies operate on blockchain technology, allowing for secure and transparent peer-to-peer transactions without the need for intermediaries like banks.

How Cryptocurrencies Work:

1. **Decentralized Network**: Cryptocurrencies operate on decentralized blockchain networks, where the blockchain serves as a public ledger for all transactions.
2. **Transactions**: Users send cryptocurrencies to one another using public keys (addresses). Each transaction is digitally signed by the sender and verified by the network before being recorded on the blockchain.
3. **Mining or Staking**: In proof-of-work systems (e.g., Bitcoin), transactions are validated by miners who solve complex mathematical puzzles. In proof-of-stake systems (e.g., Ethereum 2.0), validators are chosen based on the amount of cryptocurrency they hold and are willing to "stake" as collateral.

4. **Security**: Cryptocurrencies use cryptographic hashing algorithms (like SHA-256) to secure transactions and ensure that once data is added to the blockchain, it cannot be altered.

Popular Cryptocurrencies:

- **Bitcoin (BTC)**: The first and most well-known cryptocurrency, Bitcoin uses the Proof of Work (PoW) consensus mechanism.
- **Ethereum (ETH)**: A blockchain platform that enables smart contracts and decentralized applications (dApps), Ethereum is transitioning from Proof of Work to Proof of Stake (PoS).
- **Litecoin (LTC)**: Often referred to as the "silver to Bitcoin's gold," Litecoin offers faster transaction times and a different hashing algorithm.
- **Ripple (XRP)**: A cryptocurrency focused on facilitating fast, low-cost cross-border payments through a consensus algorithm.

3. Using Python for Cryptocurrency Data Analysis

Python, with its powerful libraries and extensive ecosystem, is well-suited for analyzing cryptocurrency data. This section will guide you through how to gather, manipulate, and visualize cryptocurrency data using Python.

a. Collecting Cryptocurrency Data:

To analyze cryptocurrency data, we first need to access it. There are several APIs available for retrieving real-time and historical cryptocurrency data.

- **CoinGecko API**: A free API that provides data on cryptocurrencies, including prices, market cap, volume, etc.
- **CryptoCompare API**: Another popular API for cryptocurrency data, including historical data and real-time market information.
- **Binance API**: A cryptocurrency exchange API that provides real-time market data, as well as trading functionality.

Example: Fetching Real-Time Cryptocurrency Data using the CoinGecko API:

python

```python
import requests

def fetch_crypto_data():
    url = "https://api.coingecko.com/api/v3/coins/bitcoin"
    response = requests.get(url)
    data = response.json()
    return data
```

```
crypto_data = fetch_crypto_data()
print("Bitcoin data:", crypto_data['name'],
crypto_data['market_data']['current_price']['usd'])
```

This code fetches data on Bitcoin, including the current price in USD.

b. Analyzing Cryptocurrency Price Trends:

Once we have access to cryptocurrency data, we can analyze it. For example, using **Pandas** to process and visualize price trends over time.

python

```
import pandas as pd
import matplotlib.pyplot as plt


# Example of fetching historical data (this would typically be done
with an API request)
data = pd.DataFrame({
    'timestamp': ['2021-01-01', '2021-02-01', '2021-03-01', '2021-04-
01'],
    'price': [29000, 34000, 43000, 56000]
})
data['timestamp'] = pd.to_datetime(data['timestamp'])
data.set_index('timestamp', inplace=True)
```

```
# Plotting the price trend
plt.plot(data.index, data['price'])
plt.title('Bitcoin Price Trend')
plt.xlabel('Date')
plt.ylabel('Price (USD)')
plt.show()
```

This code snippet creates a simple line chart showing Bitcoin price trends over time using historical data.

c. Visualizing Cryptocurrency Market Data:

For advanced visualization, you can use **Plotly** or **Seaborn** to create interactive plots. This can be useful for monitoring the performance of various cryptocurrencies, analyzing correlation, or observing market movements.

4. Building a Simple Blockchain with Python

Now that we've covered the theory and tools behind blockchain and cryptocurrencies, let's take a hands-on approach by building a basic blockchain in Python.

a. Basic Blockchain Structure:

A basic blockchain consists of blocks, each containing data (e.g., transaction details), a **timestamp**, and a **hash** of the previous block to maintain the chain's integrity.

Here's a simple implementation of a blockchain in Python:

python

```python
import hashlib
import time

class Block:
    def __init__(self, index, timestamp, data, previous_hash):
        self.index = index
        self.timestamp = timestamp
        self.data = data
        self.previous_hash = previous_hash
        self.hash = self.calculate_hash()

    def calculate_hash(self):
        block_string = f"{self.index}{self.timestamp}{self.data}{self.previous_hash}"
        return hashlib.sha256(block_string.encode()).hexdigest()

class Blockchain:
    def __init__(self):
        self.chain = [self.create_genesis_block()]

    def create_genesis_block(self):
        return Block(0, time.time(), "Genesis Block", "0")

    def add_block(self, data):
```

```
    last_block = self.chain[-1]
    new_block = Block(len(self.chain), time.time(), data,
last_block.hash)
    self.chain.append(new_block)

# Example of creating a blockchain and adding blocks
blockchain = Blockchain()
blockchain.add_block("First block of data")
blockchain.add_block("Second block of data")

# Print the blockchain
for block in blockchain.chain:
  print(f"Block {block.index} - Hash: {block.hash}")
```

In this example:

- We define a Block class that contains the block's index, timestamp, data, and a reference to the previous block's hash.
- The Blockchain class manages the chain and provides a method to add new blocks.
- We use the SHA-256 hash function to secure the blocks and ensure immutability.

5. Real-World Applications of Blockchain and Cryptocurrencies

Blockchain and cryptocurrencies have far-reaching implications beyond just digital currency. Some key applications include:

- **Supply Chain Management**: Blockchain enables transparent tracking of goods from origin to destination, ensuring authenticity and reducing fraud.
- **Smart Contracts**: Built on blockchain platforms like Ethereum, smart contracts are self-executing contracts with predefined rules that automatically execute when conditions are met.
- **Decentralized Finance (DeFi)**: Using blockchain and cryptocurrencies, DeFi allows users to access financial services (like lending, borrowing, and trading) without intermediaries.
- **Voting Systems**: Blockchain can be used to create secure, transparent, and tamper-proof voting systems.
- **Identity Management**: Blockchain technology can provide secure and decentralized identity systems, reducing the risk of identity theft and fraud.

Blockchain and cryptocurrencies are at the forefront of a technological revolution, reshaping industries by enabling decentralized, secure, and transparent transactions. Understanding the algorithms and data structures behind these technologies is key to unlocking their potential. With the knowledge gained in this chapter, you can begin to experiment with blockchain-based projects and analyze cryptocurrency data using Python, opening the door to a wealth of opportunities in the growing field of blockchain development.

CHAPTER 22: ADVANCED MACHINE LEARNING IN FINANCE

The financial industry has increasingly embraced machine learning (ML) and artificial intelligence (AI) for applications ranging from algorithmic trading to fraud detection and credit risk assessment. Machine learning provides powerful tools for analyzing large datasets, identifying patterns, and making predictions in ways that were once impossible with traditional financial models. This chapter will dive into advanced machine learning techniques specifically tailored for financial applications, including deep learning, time series forecasting with Long Short-Term Memory (LSTM) networks, and reinforcement learning for developing adaptive trading strategies.

By the end of this chapter, you will have a deeper understanding of how advanced machine learning techniques can be applied to finance, and you will have practical knowledge of how to implement these algorithms using Python.

1. Deep Learning in Financial Analysis

Deep learning, a subset of machine learning that involves multi-layered neural networks, has shown tremendous promise in fields such as image recognition, natural language processing, and financial forecasting. In finance, deep learning is used for tasks like fraud detection, risk modeling, and predicting market trends.

a. What is Deep Learning?

Deep learning models consist of layers of neurons (artificial nodes) that mimic the way the human brain processes information. These models can automatically learn features from raw data, eliminating the need for manual feature engineering.

The most common types of deep learning models are:

- **Feedforward Neural Networks (FNN)**: These are simple, fully connected neural networks that pass data through multiple layers. In finance, these networks are used for credit scoring and predictive analytics.
- **Convolutional Neural Networks (CNN)**: Although typically used for image analysis, CNNs have been applied to financial data (like charts) for pattern recognition.
- **Recurrent Neural Networks (RNN)**: These networks are specifically designed for sequence prediction tasks and are particularly useful for time series forecasting in finance, such as stock price prediction or volatility forecasting.

b. Practical Application: Predicting Stock Prices Using a Neural Network

In this example, we use a basic feedforward neural network to predict stock prices using historical data.

python

```python
import numpy as np
import pandas as pd
from sklearn.model_selection import train_test_split
from sklearn.preprocessing import MinMaxScaler
from keras.models import Sequential
from keras.layers import Dense


# Load historical stock data (example CSV with Date and Close columns)
data = pd.read_csv('stock_data.csv')
data = data[['Close']]   # We're predicting stock price based on closing value


# Scale the data
scaler = MinMaxScaler(feature_range=(0, 1))
scaled_data = scaler.fit_transform(data)


# Prepare training data
X = []
y = []
for i in range(60, len(scaled_data)):   # Use 60 previous days to predict next day's price
    X.append(scaled_data[i-60:i, 0])
    y.append(scaled_data[i, 0])
```

```
X = np.array(X)
y = np.array(y)

# Train-test split
X_train, X_test, y_train, y_test = train_test_split(X, y,
test_size=0.2, shuffle=False)

# Build and train a simple neural network model
model = Sequential()
model.add(Dense(units=64, activation='relu', input_dim=60))
model.add(Dense(units=32, activation='relu'))
model.add(Dense(units=1))   # Output layer for predicting stock
price

model.compile(optimizer='adam', loss='mean_squared_error')
model.fit(X_train, y_train, epochs=10, batch_size=32)

# Predict on test data
predicted_prices = model.predict(X_test)
```

In this example, we prepare the stock data by scaling it and using the previous 60 days' closing prices to predict the next day's closing price. The model is a simple feedforward neural network with one hidden layer, and it's trained using the Adam optimizer.

2. Time Series Forecasting with LSTM Networks

Time series forecasting is a crucial application in finance, particularly for predicting stock prices, interest rates, or market volatility. Traditional models like ARIMA are effective for linear time series data, but they struggle with more complex, non-linear patterns. LSTM networks, a type of recurrent neural network (RNN), are specifically designed to handle sequential data and are better at capturing long-term dependencies in time series data.

a. What is LSTM?

LSTM (Long Short-Term Memory) is a type of RNN that has a specialized structure to retain long-term memory and avoid the vanishing gradient problem, which occurs in traditional RNNs when learning long sequences. LSTMs are particularly useful for financial time series data because they can capture long-term dependencies in stock prices or financial metrics.

b. Practical Application: Stock Price Prediction with LSTM

python

```
from keras.models import Sequential
from keras.layers import LSTM, Dense, Dropout
from sklearn.preprocessing import MinMaxScaler

# Load and preprocess the data
data = pd.read_csv('stock_data.csv')
```

```
data = data[['Close']]
scaler = MinMaxScaler(feature_range=(0, 1))
scaled_data = scaler.fit_transform(data)

# Prepare the data for LSTM input (60 days lookback)
X, y = [], []
for i in range(60, len(scaled_data)):
    X.append(scaled_data[i-60:i, 0])
    y.append(scaled_data[i, 0])

X = np.array(X)
y = np.array(y)

# Reshape X to be compatible with LSTM input
X = X.reshape(X.shape[0], X.shape[1], 1)

# Split into train and test sets
X_train, X_test, y_train, y_test = train_test_split(X, y,
test_size=0.2, shuffle=False)

# Build the LSTM model
model = Sequential()
model.add(LSTM(units=100,           return_sequences=True,
input_shape=(X_train.shape[1], 1)))
model.add(Dropout(0.2))
```

```
model.add(LSTM(units=100, return_sequences=False))
model.add(Dropout(0.2))
model.add(Dense(units=1))

# Compile and train the model
model.compile(optimizer='adam', loss='mean_squared_error')
model.fit(X_train, y_train, epochs=10, batch_size=32)

# Predict future stock prices
predicted_prices = model.predict(X_test)
```

In this example, the LSTM network is used to predict future stock prices based on the previous 60 days of data. The data is preprocessed and scaled to a range between 0 and 1, as LSTMs generally perform better with normalized data. After training the model, it is used to predict stock prices on the test data.

3. Reinforcement Learning for Trading Strategies

Reinforcement learning (RL) is a branch of machine learning where an agent learns to make decisions by interacting with its environment. In the context of finance, RL can be used to develop adaptive trading strategies that maximize profits and minimize risks based on feedback from the market.

a. What is Reinforcement Learning?

In reinforcement learning, the agent learns by taking actions and receiving rewards or penalties based on the outcomes of those actions. The goal is to learn a policy (a mapping from states to actions) that maximizes cumulative rewards over time.

b. Reinforcement Learning in Trading

In trading, RL algorithms can be used to create systems that decide when to buy, sell, or hold assets. The model receives data (like stock prices and indicators) and learns to optimize its trading strategy based on the reward function (e.g., profit or loss).

c. Practical Example: Simple Q-learning for Trading

python

```python
import numpy as np
import random

class QLearningTrader:
    def __init__(self, num_actions=3, num_states=100):
        self.q_table = np.zeros((num_states, num_actions))  # Q-table initialized to zeros
        self.num_actions = num_actions
        self.learning_rate = 0.1
        self.discount_factor = 0.9
        self.exploration_rate = 1.0

    def choose_action(self, state):
        if random.uniform(0, 1) < self.exploration_rate:
```

```python
        return random.randint(0, self.num_actions - 1)    # Exploration: random action
        return np.argmax(self.q_table[state])  # Exploitation: choose best known action


    def update_q_table(self, state, action, reward, next_state):
        best_next_action = np.argmax(self.q_table[next_state])
        self.q_table[state, action] += self.learning_rate * (reward + self.discount_factor * self.q_table[next_state, best_next_action] - self.q_table[state, action])


# Example of using Q-learning for trading (simplified)
trader = QLearningTrader()


# Simulating a simple trading environment
state = 50  # Example state (could be based on technical indicators)
action = trader.choose_action(state)  # Choose an action (buy, sell, hold)
reward = random.random()  # Reward (e.g., profit or loss)
next_state = 51   # New state after action (could be new price or indicator)


# Update Q-table based on the reward
trader.update_q_table(state, action, reward, next_state)
```

This example uses Q-learning, a popular reinforcement learning algorithm, to make decisions in a simplified trading environment. The model's actions (buy, sell, or hold) are based on its learned policy, which is updated using the Q-table after each trade.

4. Challenges and Considerations

While machine learning offers tremendous potential for financial applications, several challenges must be addressed:

- **Data Quality**: Financial data is often noisy and incomplete, which can hinder model performance. Proper data cleaning and feature engineering are essential.

- **Overfitting**: Machine learning models can easily overfit to historical data, leading to poor performance in real-world scenarios. Regularization techniques, cross-validation, and out-of-sample testing can help mitigate this risk.

- **Interpretability**: Many machine learning models, particularly deep learning models, are often seen as "black boxes." In finance, where interpretability is crucial for regulatory and decision-making purposes, techniques such as SHAP (Shapley Additive Explanations) can help explain model predictions.

- **Computational Resources**: Advanced machine learning models, especially deep learning, can be computationally expensive. It is essential to ensure that the infrastructure is in place to handle large-scale financial data efficiently.

Advanced machine learning techniques like deep learning, LSTM networks, and reinforcement learning are transforming the finance industry by enabling smarter predictions, more adaptive trading strategies, and better decision-making tools. By leveraging Python and popular ML libraries, you can begin to build powerful models that can analyze complex financial data and unlock new opportunities for profitability and efficiency in the financial sector.

CHAPTER 23: REAL-TIME FINANCIAL ANALYSIS

Real-time financial analysis is essential in today's fast-paced financial markets. The ability to process and analyze data as it is generated—whether from stock prices, transaction records, or news feeds—enables traders, analysts, and institutions to make decisions based on the most current information available. In this chapter, we will explore how real-time data analysis is integrated into financial systems and how Python can be used to build applications that process and visualize financial data in real-time.

By the end of this chapter, you will understand how to collect and process live market data, build real-time dashboards, and integrate real-time financial analysis into your decision-making process.

1. Introduction to Real-Time Financial Analysis

Real-time financial analysis refers to the process of continuously gathering and analyzing financial data to make decisions or generate insights without delays. This capability is critical in markets like stocks, forex, commodities, and cryptocurrencies, where even seconds of delay can result in significant gains or losses.

In a traditional financial analysis system, data is collected over time and processed in batches. However, in real-time systems, data is processed as it comes in, often with minimal delay (latency). This requires specialized architectures, data pipelines, and tools to ensure that the analysis is both fast and accurate.

Real-Time Data Sources in Finance:

- **Stock and Market Data Feeds:** Real-time stock prices, exchange rates, and commodity prices.
- **Financial News and Sentiment Data:** News articles, tweets, and other textual data that could influence markets.
- **Transaction and Trading Data:** Real-time trades and market orders from exchanges.
- **Sensor Data:** For quantitative trading, data from sensors might also be processed in real-time.

These data sources are usually streamed to an application or system that processes them, often in near real-time, to produce insights, alerts, or actions.

2. Using Python for Real-Time Financial Data Analysis

Python, with its rich ecosystem of libraries, is a perfect tool for building real-time financial applications. Libraries like pandas, numpy, and matplotlib are useful for data manipulation and visualization, while specialized libraries like Kafka, Twisted, and AsyncIO allow handling of real-time data streams.

a. Real-Time Data Collection and Streaming

To collect live financial data, we typically interact with APIs provided by financial institutions, brokers, or data vendors. Popular sources for real-time market data include:

- **Yahoo Finance API**
- **Alpha Vantage**
- **Quandl (now part of Nasdaq Data Link)**
- **Crypto exchanges (e.g., Binance, Kraken) for cryptocurrency data**

Example: Collecting Real-Time Stock Data from Yahoo Finance with yfinance

The yfinance library can be used to collect stock data in real-time for analysis. While it may not offer truly "real-time" tick-by-tick data, it can pull live data with a slight delay.

python

```
import yfinance as yf
import time

# Define the stock ticker symbol
ticker = 'AAPL'

while True:
    # Get live stock data
```

```
stock = yf.Ticker(ticker)
live_data = stock.history(period='1d', interval='1m')  # 1-minute
```
intervals for real-time data

```
# Print live data
print(live_data.tail(1))  # Print most recent data
```

```
time.sleep(60)  # Wait 60 seconds before fetching new data
```
In this example, we continuously fetch 1-minute interval stock data for Apple (AAPL) and display the most recent data every minute.

b. Real-Time Data Pipelines

For more complex use cases, such as high-frequency trading or real-time risk assessment, data pipelines are often required to handle large volumes of data. Frameworks like Apache Kafka or RabbitMQ can manage streams of data and ensure it is processed in real-time. Python interfaces like kafka-python allow you to interact with such systems.

Example: Integrating with Kafka for Real-Time Data

Kafka is a distributed event streaming platform often used for real-time data pipelines. You can consume real-time market data streams and process them in Python using kafka-python.

python

```
from kafka import KafkaConsumer
```

```
import json

# Connect to Kafka
consumer = KafkaConsumer(
    'market_data',  # Kafka topic
    bootstrap_servers=['localhost:9092'],  # Kafka server
    auto_offset_reset='earliest',  # Start from the earliest message
    group_id='financial-analysis'
)

for message in consumer:
    data = json.loads(message.value.decode('utf-8'))
    print(f"New Market Data: {data}")
```

In this example, we consume data from a Kafka topic called market_data. Every time a new message (market data) arrives, it is processed by the Python consumer.

---

3. Building Real-Time Dashboards and Visualizations

Visualizing real-time financial data is an essential part of monitoring financial performance, trends, and market conditions. Dashboards allow stakeholders to view key metrics in real time, enabling them to make informed decisions.

a. Interactive Dashboards with Dash

Dash is a Python framework for building web-based dashboards, especially useful for real-time financial data visualization. Dash apps can handle dynamic visualizations such as updating stock prices, price change percentages, and real-time charts.

Here's a simple example of creating a real-time stock price dashboard using Dash and Plotly:

python

```
import dash
from dash import dcc, html
import plotly.graph_objs as go
import yfinance as yf
import dash.dependencies as dd
import time


# Initialize the Dash app
app = dash.Dash(__name__)


# Define the app layout
app.layout = html.Div([
    html.H1('Real-Time Stock Data'),
    dcc.Graph(id='live-graph'),
    dcc.Interval(id='graph-update', interval=60000, n_intervals=0)
# Update every minute
```

```
])


# Function to fetch live stock data
def get_stock_data():
    ticker = 'AAPL'
    stock = yf.Ticker(ticker)
    live_data = stock.history(period='1d', interval='1m')  # 1-minute
interval
    return live_data


# Define callback to update the graph
@app.callback(
    dd.Output('live-graph', 'figure'),
    [dd.Input('graph-update', 'n_intervals')]
)
def update_graph(n):
    data = get_stock_data()
    trace = go.Scatter(
        x=data.index, y=data['Close'],
        mode='lines', name='AAPL Stock Price'
    )
    return {'data': [trace], 'layout': go.Layout(title='Live   Stock
Price')}


# Run the app
```

```
if __name__ == '__main__':
    app.run_server(debug=True)
```

In this example, we create a Dash app that pulls the latest stock data every minute and updates the graph accordingly. You can visualize the stock price trend live, which can be very useful in trading applications.

b. Real-Time Alerts and Notifications

In a financial system, real-time alerts are essential for notifying users of important events, such as a price crossing a threshold or an abnormal pattern detected in the data. Alerts can be sent via email, SMS, or other communication channels.

To set up real-time alerts in Python, you can use the smtplib module for email notifications, twilio for SMS alerts, or third-party services like Slack or Telegram.

Here's a simple example of sending an email alert when a stock price exceeds a certain threshold:

python

```
import smtplib
from email.mime.text import MIMEText
from email.mime.multipart import MIMEMultipart

# Define email details
```

```python
def send_email(subject, body, recipient_email):
    sender_email = "your_email@example.com"
    password = "your_password"

    msg = MIMEMultipart()
    msg['From'] = sender_email
    msg['To'] = recipient_email
    msg['Subject'] = subject
    msg.attach(MIMEText(body, 'plain'))

    # Connect to the email server and send the email
    server = smtplib.SMTP('smtp.gmail.com', 587)
    server.starttls()
    server.login(sender_email, password)
    text = msg.as_string()
    server.sendmail(sender_email, recipient_email, text)
    server.quit()


# Check stock price and send email alert if threshold is exceeded
price_threshold = 1500
stock = yf.Ticker('AAPL')
price = stock.history(period='1d')['Close'][-1]

if price > price_threshold:
```

send_email('Stock Price Alert', f'AAPL stock price has exceeded {price_threshold}.   Current   price: {price}', 'recipient@example.com')

In this example, we send an email alert whenever the stock price exceeds a specified threshold.

4. Integrating Real-Time Market Data into Financial Models

In many financial models, particularly in quantitative trading, the ability to incorporate real-time market data is crucial for making timely and informed decisions. Real-time market data feeds can be used to update portfolio valuations, adjust risk models, or trigger trading signals based on market movements.

Example: Adaptive Risk Management System

Real-time data can be integrated into a risk management model to assess the current risk of a portfolio. As market data changes, such as changes in stock prices, volatility, or interest rates, the model can dynamically update risk metrics (e.g., Value at Risk or VaR).

5. Challenges in Real-Time Financial Analysis

While the benefits of real-time financial analysis are clear, there are several challenges to consider:

- **Latency:** Real-time systems need to minimize latency (delays) to ensure that the analysis reflects the most current data. High-frequency trading, for example, often requires microsecond-level latency.

- **Data Quality:** Real-time data can be noisy or incomplete. Ensuring data quality in real-time systems is crucial for making accurate predictions and decisions.
- **Scalability:** Handling large volumes of data efficiently is necessary, especially in high-frequency trading environments.
- **Infrastructure:** Real-time systems require robust and scalable infrastructure. Distributed systems, cloud computing, and edge computing are often necessary to support real-time financial applications.

Real-time financial analysis has become a cornerstone of modern trading and decision-making. By using Python, we can collect, process, and analyze live data to create dashboards, alert systems, and predictive models that support real-time decision-making in financial markets. While there are challenges to overcome, the ability to process and react to data in real-time opens up new possibilities for financial analysis, risk management, and trading strategies.

CHAPTER 24: ALGORITHMS IN PRACTICE: REAL-WORLD APPLICATIONS

Algorithms are at the heart of many industries today, powering everything from search engines to social media platforms to autonomous vehicles. In this final chapter, we'll explore real-world use cases where algorithms play a critical role, focusing on their practical applications in various fields such as e-commerce, healthcare, fintech, and beyond. By studying these examples, you will gain insight into how to implement the algorithms you've learned about in this book and adapt them to solve complex, real-world problems.

We'll also examine how algorithms enable businesses to scale their systems, improve user experiences, and optimize operations, with a focus on efficiency, accuracy, and speed.

1. Case Studies: Algorithms in E-Commerce, Healthcare, and Fintech

Understanding how algorithms power real-world systems can help you appreciate their versatility and importance in today's data-driven world. Let's take a look at how different industries leverage algorithms to optimize processes and deliver value to users.

a. E-Commerce: Personalization and Recommendation Systems

In e-commerce, algorithms are primarily used to personalize the shopping experience and recommend products that a user is likely to purchase. Recommendation systems are built using algorithms that analyze user behavior, past purchases, browsing history, and other data to predict which products will interest the user.

Algorithms used in e-commerce:

- **Collaborative Filtering:** This is one of the most common techniques for building recommendation systems. Collaborative filtering uses the behavior of users who are similar to a target user to recommend products they might like. For example, Amazon's "Customers who bought this also bought" feature.

- **Content-Based Filtering:** This method recommends items based on their similarity to products the user has liked in the past. If a user frequently buys books on machine learning, they might be recommended more books on similar topics.

- **Matrix Factorization:** A popular approach for collaborative filtering, matrix factorization involves decomposing large matrices of user-item interactions into smaller, more manageable matrices that represent user preferences and item features.

Example: Building a Simple Recommendation System in Python

python

```python
import pandas as pd
from sklearn.metrics.pairwise import cosine_similarity

# Sample user-item interaction data
data = {'user': ['Alice', 'Bob', 'Charlie', 'David', 'Eve'],
    'item': ['Laptop', 'Smartphone', 'Tablet', 'Smartwatch',
'Laptop'],
    'rating': [5, 4, 3, 5, 4]}

df = pd.DataFrame(data)

# Creating a user-item matrix
user_item_matrix = df.pivot_table(index='user', columns='item',
values='rating', fill_value=0)

# Compute cosine similarity between users
cos_sim = cosine_similarity(user_item_matrix)
sim_matrix                =                pd.DataFrame(cos_sim,
index=user_item_matrix.index, columns=user_item_matrix.index)

# Show similarity matrix
```

print(sim_matrix)

In this example, we calculate the cosine similarity between users based on their interactions with various items. Such recommendation algorithms are widely used by e-commerce platforms like Amazon, Netflix, and Spotify to enhance user engagement.

b. Healthcare: Predictive Models for Disease Diagnosis

In healthcare, algorithms are increasingly used to predict and diagnose diseases, improve patient outcomes, and optimize resource management. Machine learning algorithms can analyze large amounts of medical data, such as patient histories, lab results, and genetic information, to predict conditions like cancer, diabetes, and heart disease.

Algorithms used in healthcare:

- **Logistic Regression:** Often used for binary classification problems, such as predicting the likelihood of a patient developing a disease.
- **Random Forests:** A popular ensemble learning technique used for classification and regression, which is especially useful for medical diagnosis.
- **Neural Networks:** Deep learning techniques, particularly convolutional neural networks (CNNs), are used for analyzing medical images, such as detecting tumors in radiology images.

Example: Predicting Disease with Logistic Regression

python

```python
import pandas as pd
from sklearn.model_selection import train_test_split
from sklearn.linear_model import LogisticRegression
from sklearn.metrics import accuracy_score

# Sample dataset: Patient data with features (age, blood pressure,
etc.) and target (disease)
data = pd.DataFrame({
    'age': [25, 45, 35, 50, 60],
    'blood_pressure': [120, 140, 130, 145, 160],
    'cholesterol': [200, 250, 220, 240, 270],
    'disease': [0, 1, 0, 1, 1]  # 0 = No, 1 = Yes
})

# Features and target
X = data[['age', 'blood_pressure', 'cholesterol']]
y = data['disease']

# Train/test split
X_train, X_test, y_train, y_test = train_test_split(X, y,
test_size=0.2, random_state=42)
```

```
# Logistic regression model
model = LogisticRegression()
model.fit(X_train, y_train)
```

```
# Predictions
y_pred = model.predict(X_test)
```

```
# Evaluate accuracy
accuracy = accuracy_score(y_test, y_pred)
print(f"Accuracy: {accuracy:.2f}")
```

This example demonstrates a simple logistic regression model used to predict whether a patient has a particular disease based on certain health metrics. In real-world applications, such models are trained on large datasets to provide diagnostic assistance to healthcare professionals.

c. Fintech: Fraud Detection and Risk Assessment

In fintech, algorithms are essential for detecting fraudulent activities, assessing credit risk, and managing investments. Machine learning algorithms, in particular, are used to identify patterns of behavior that may indicate fraud or to assess the likelihood of loan defaults.

Algorithms used in fintech:

- **Anomaly Detection:** Algorithms like Isolation Forest and One-Class SVM are used to detect unusual patterns that could indicate fraud in transactions.
- **Decision Trees:** Used for assessing the risk associated with lending money, decision trees help model the relationship between various factors (e.g., income, credit history) and the likelihood of default.
- **Neural Networks:** Used for more complex tasks such as pattern recognition in large-scale financial transactions.

Example: Fraud Detection with Anomaly Detection Algorithm

python

```python
import numpy as np
from sklearn.ensemble import IsolationForest

# Simulate transactional data (e.g., purchase amount)
transaction_data = np.array([[100], [200], [300], [400], [10000]])

# Train an anomaly detection model
model = IsolationForest(contamination=0.1)   # Assume 10% of transactions are fraudulent
model.fit(transaction_data)

# Predict anomalies (fraudulent transactions)
predictions = model.predict(transaction_data)
```

-1 indicates an anomaly (fraudulent transaction), 1 indicates normal transaction

print(predictions)

This example uses the IsolationForest algorithm to detect fraudulent transactions based on their unusual values. Such systems are widely used in financial institutions to flag suspicious activity and prevent fraud.

2. Building Scalable Systems with Efficient Algorithms

As your application scales—whether you're running an e-commerce website, a healthcare platform, or a financial trading system—the efficiency of your algorithms becomes more important. Systems that work perfectly for small-scale applications can quickly fall apart when faced with large amounts of data, thousands of users, or millions of transactions. Scalable systems are built using algorithms that are optimized for both time and space efficiency.

Key considerations for building scalable systems:

- **Distributed Systems:** Distributed algorithms allow tasks to be split across multiple machines, improving scalability and reliability.

- **Data Structures for Scalability:** Data structures such as hash tables, balanced trees, and graphs are often used to organize and retrieve large datasets quickly.

- **Load Balancing and Caching:** Algorithms for distributing workloads efficiently and storing frequently accessed data in memory can dramatically improve performance.

Example: Caching with LRU (Least Recently Used) Algorithm

python

```python
from collections import OrderedDict

class LRUCache:
    def __init__(self, capacity: int):
        self.cache = OrderedDict()
        self.capacity = capacity

    def get(self, key: int) -> int:
        if key not in self.cache:
            return -1
        else:
            # Move the accessed item to the end of the OrderedDict
            self.cache.move_to_end(key)
            return self.cache[key]

    def put(self, key: int, value: int) -> None:
        if key in self.cache:
            # Remove the old value
            self.cache.move_to_end(key)
```

```
        self.cache[key] = value

        if len(self.cache) > self.capacity:
            # Remove the first (least recently used) item
            self.cache.popitem(last=False)


# Create an LRU cache with capacity of 3
lru_cache = LRUCache(3)
lru_cache.put(1, 1)
lru_cache.put(2, 2)
print(lru_cache.get(1))  # returns 1
lru_cache.put(3, 3)
lru_cache.put(4, 4)  # evicts key 2
print(lru_cache.get(2))  # returns -1
```

In this example, an LRU (Least Recently Used) cache is implemented to store the most recently accessed items, efficiently evicting the least recently used items when the cache exceeds its capacity. This algorithm is widely used in systems that need to optimize memory usage and performance, such as web servers and databases.

3. The Future of Algorithms: AI and Quantum Computing

As algorithms continue to evolve, their applications will become even more complex and impactful. Two areas that hold significant promise for the future of algorithms are **artificial intelligence (AI)** and **quantum computing**.

- **Artificial Intelligence:** Algorithms are at the core of AI systems, enabling machines to learn from data and make decisions. Machine learning, deep learning, and reinforcement learning are all built on powerful algorithms that can adapt and improve over time.

- **Quantum Computing:** Quantum computers have the potential to solve certain problems far faster than classical computers by leveraging quantum bits (qubits). Quantum algorithms could revolutionize fields like cryptography, optimization, and complex simulations.

4. Practical Advice for Choosing and Implementing Algorithms

Choosing the right algorithm for a problem is critical to ensuring that your system is efficient, scalable, and maintainable. Here are some practical tips:

- **Understand the Problem:** Take time to understand the problem domain and the requirements of the system you're building before selecting an algorithm.

- **Analyze the Complexity:** Always consider the time and space complexity of the algorithms you're choosing, especially when dealing with large datasets.

- **Test and Optimize:** Algorithms may need to be tuned and optimized based on the specific constraints and data of your application.

- **Keep It Simple:** Start with simple, well-understood algorithms and only introduce complexity when necessary.

Algorithms are the backbone of modern technology, and their applications span virtually every industry. From recommendation systems in e-commerce to disease diagnosis in healthcare and fraud detection in finance, the practical use cases for algorithms are vast and growing. Understanding how to choose, implement, and optimize algorithms is an essential skill for any software engineer or data scientist. By studying real-world examples, building scalable systems, and exploring the cutting-edge technologies of AI and quantum computing, we can ensure that algorithms continue to drive innovation and solve complex challenges in the future.

www.ingramcontent.com/pod-product-compliance
Lightning Source LLC
LaVergne TN
LVHW022340060326
832902LV00022B/4154